MIGRATION

MIGRATION

EXPLORING THE REMARKABLE
JOURNEYS OF BIRDS

Hardie Grant

QUADRILLE

Publishing Director Sarah Lavelle
Commissioning Editor Harriet Butt
Senior Designer Nikki Ellis, Maeve Bargman
Illustrator Katy Christianson
Head of Production Stephen Lang
Production Controller Katie Jarvis

Published in 2020 by Quadrille,
an imprint of Hardie Grant Publishing

Quadrille
52–54 Southwark Street
London SE1 1UN
quadrille.com

Cataloguing in Publication Data: a catalogue record for
this book is available from the British Library.

ISBN 978 1 78713 504 8

Printed in China

FSC
www.fsc.org
MIX
Paper from
responsible sources
FSC® C020056

CONTENTS

A NOTE ABOUT BIRD NAMES

Wherever a bird is mentioned, both its most familiar common name and its scientific name are included to ensure clarity. There are, for example, 120 bird species that could be called 'robin' but there is only one Indian robin (*Saxicoloides fulicatus*). While both names may change over time depending on range, local customs and scientific reclassification, those given in this book were accurate at the time of writing and conform to accepted names from BirdLife International.

European Robin
(*Erithacus rubecula*)

INTRODUCTION

I have always loved birds, and growing up in northern
Michigan, I was constantly aware of their seasonal travels.
In particular, the American robin (*Turdus migratorius*)
– Michigan's state bird and a common visitor to my
childhood yard – would come and go with the snowfall,
leaving as the snows deepened and not returning
until spring.

As I began my own journeys in life, I discovered more birds
and learned more about their movements. I met my first
cattle egret (*Bubulcus ibis*) during my freshman year of
college, ogled a swallow-tailed kite (*Elanoides forficatus*)
from the balcony of an early apartment, and welcomed
lazuli buntings (*Passerina amoena*) to feeders at my first
house. Each one taught me a bit more about birds and how
they moved, and the more I travelled myself, the more
I learned about birds' journeys and migration.

I've been fortunate that my own travels have been frequent
and widespread. My personal migrations have happened
during every month of the year, via every mode of
transportation, and have moved me not only around my
own country, but to far-flung destinations in the Pacific
Islands, Caribbean, Middle East, Central America
and Europe.

Along the way I have seen some truly spectacular birds,
from a golden eagle (*Aquila chrysaetos*) yawning alongside
a wooded canyon trail in Utah, to a laysan albatross
(*Phoebastria immutabilis*) calmly soaring just feet above
my head on a jutting cliff in Hawaii. I'll never forget my
first Eurasian spoonbill (*Platalea leucorodia*), flying north
from the Red Sea into Israel, or the Italian sparrow (*Passer
italiae*) I saw at Autogrill outside Florence.

Writing *Migration: Exploring the Remarkable Journeys of Birds* has given me many opportunities to fly further into the world of birds' travels. Just as I've had to change routes and adjust plans, I've learned how birds adapt to their different journeys, and how migration is much more than just the seasonal north–south travels I noted in my youth. I've also learned that the cancelled flights, changed itineraries and bad weather I've encountered are nothing compared to the hardships birds face during migration, or to the risks that put their future movements in jeopardy.

It is my hope that everyone who reads this book will not only be inspired to make journeys of their own to see more spectacular birds, but also to take steps to safeguard all birds' migrations. Each of us ought to have the chance to see some of the species featured in these pages and experience the wonders of birds' movements at all times of year.

Let's fly.

♂ Laysan Albatross
(Phoebastria immutabilis)

WHAT IS MIGRATION?

Simply defined, migration is movement. But it is so much more than that.

Birds are moving all the time. They fly in different ways depending on whether they're foraging, visiting water sources, gathering nesting material, escaping predators or chasing intruders. They have special types of flight to entice mates and to show off their strength to competitors. Some birds, such as the barn swallow (*Hirundo rustica*), fly while drinking, and others, such as the peregrine falcon (*Falco peregrinus*), make spectacular aerial dives while hunting. These flights are all beautiful, graceful movements, but none are migration.

From the Latin *migratus*, the word migration refers not just to movement, but also to a significant geographic change. Migration is when an entire population undertakes a semi-permanent, seasonal relocation. But just how permanent, how seasonal, and how far that geographic shift is can vary greatly.

There are approximately 10,000 bird species in the world, and more than half of them are considered migratory to some degree. Yet not one of those more than 5,000 species migrates in exactly the same way, at exactly the same time, or along exactly the same route to exactly the same destination.

Barn Swallow
(*Hirundo rustica*)

STUDYING MIGRATION

Humans have been fascinated by migration for more than 3,000 years, and have studied the movements of birds ever since they first noticed their seasonal travels.

Migration is part of ancient Polynesian legends and is noted in the Old Testament of the Bible. Greek and Roman scholars studied migration, including Homer, Aristotle and Pliny the Elder. Depictions of migratory bird flocks, including the greater white-fronted goose (*Anser albifrons*), are even found in ancient Egyptian paintings and bas-relief carvings.

Today, naturalists and ornithologists around the world continue to study migration. After centuries of observations and deductions, we know a great deal about these bird movements, but there is still more we don't completely understand. Even today, migration continues to be a mysterious, stunning spectacle that fascinates, awes and inspires birders and non-birders alike.

ARCTIC TERN ♂♀
(Sterna paradisaea)

TYPE OF MIGRATION:
Seasonal, Latitudinal

Without a doubt, the Arctic tern is the record-holder for furthest-migrating bird on the planet. These endurance fliers migrate from pole to pole, a round trip that ranges from 40,000 to 72,000 kilometres (25,000 to 45,000 miles), depending on where each bird begins and ends its journey and whether you measure it by straight-line flight or by the meandering route they tend to take based on prevailing wind currents. This epic flight gives Arctic terns two summers to

enjoy – one in the Arctic and one in the Antarctic – and because of this, these birds see more daylight each year than any other creature on the planet. Even more impressive is that when the Arctic tern's long lifespan (25–30 years) is considered, an individual bird may fly more than 1 million kilometres (650,000 miles) in its lifetime – the equivalent of travelling from the earth to the moon nearly three times.

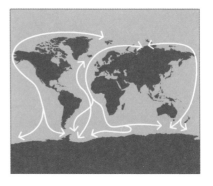

WHY BIRDS MIGRATE

Why do birds undertake their remarkable journeys at all? No bird travels to start a new job, avoid religious persecution, escape political turmoil, or for the sheer enjoyment of experiencing new places and cultures.

In fact, migration is not a conscious choice for birds at all, and they don't make any calculated decision to migrate. Rather, migration is an instinctive adaptation for survival, and those birds with that adaptation are irresistibly compelled to set forth. Two key reasons drive this instinct: food and reproduction.

In tropical regions food is plentiful year-round, from burgeoning insect life to juicy fruit, nectar-rich flowers and prey such as lizards, amphibians, small mammals and fish. But these areas are also home to many different species of birds and other wildlife all competing for the same resources. Migration, then, is how bird populations spread out to other regions to find different food sources when they need them most: when they are raising chicks.

In mid- and upper-latitude habitats, such as forests, prairies, tundras and grasslands, food availability is much more cyclical, with clear seasons of plenty and deprivation. In spring, tree buds swell, flowers bloom and insects hatch, creating new, rich food sources. This is the time when birds migrate to those bountiful areas, taking advantage of the new foods and greater amounts of space to nest and raise their young. In areas where food is more abundant, birds are able to lay larger broods and hatch more chicks, and more of those chicks will be well fed enough to survive to maturity.

During the summer, these temporary food sources continue to swell, with seeds, grains, fruits, berries and nuts ripening and sustaining wildlife, including birds. At this time of great abundance, bird populations are also at their highest as clutches hatch into young birds with hearty appetites to satiate.

But in late fall and winter these regions become much more barren. From then on, food sources will not be replenished again until the following spring. As the sources of sustenance vanish, birds need to migrate again, returning to tropical regions where they will be more crowded, but where the year-round food supplies have been restocked during the summer.

The food-abundance cycle is easy enough to see, but more difficult to understand is why reproduction should be a reason for birds to migrate. After all, many adult birds abandon their young as soon as the chicks are able to feed themselves, and many parent birds migrate well before their offspring, leaving the youngsters to attempt their first challenging migration without guidance or assistance. However, it is exactly because the young birds have been raised in a rich environment with plentiful food that they are strong enough to survive and undertake this journey on their own.

WHICH YOUNG BIRDS MIGRATE ON THEIR OWN?

Any parent knows travelling with youngsters can be a challenge. But what if you had not one or two, but four, five or even more young children to travel with? What if the trip lasted not a few minutes or hours, but days, weeks or even months? What if you weren't just going to the store, visiting a relative or taking a vacation, but completely relocating your life twice a year?

Such taxing trips are exactly what many migratory birds face just a few weeks after their chicks hatch. While many travel in family flocks that help safeguard young birds, others leave their offspring behind to face that first perilous migration on their own.

Age-differentiated migration – when mature, adult birds travel at different times than younger birds – is more common than once believed. In fact, there are hundreds of bird species that migrate differently based on age, often because adult birds are more experienced and better able to migrate faster and more efficiently than less seasoned young birds. A few of the species well known to migrate at different times according to age include:

· **Blackpoll warbler** (*Setophaga striata*)
· **Common cuckoo** (*Cuculus canorus*)
· **Common kingfisher** (*Alcedo atthis*)
· **Grey catbird** (*Dumetella carolinensis*)
· **Ruby-crowned kinglet** (*Regulus calendula*)
· **Rufous hummingbird** (*Selasphorus rufus*)
· **Savannah sparrow** (*Passerculus sandwichensis*)
· **Western sandpiper** (*Calidris mauri*)

Common Cuckoo
(*Cuculus canorus*)

While age-differentiated migration is not well documented among many specific species because of the difficulties in ageing and sexing migratory birds, it's believed to be widespread among many types of songbirds. Brood parasites – birds that lay their eggs in 'foster' nests and leave their chicks to be raised by another species – also commonly migrate without their young, given that they have no role in bringing them up. Many solo migrants do not stay in family groups past the nesting period, and will likewise migrate more quickly as adults than as juveniles.

Even before migration begins, adult birds have more fully developed digestive systems and better knowledge of the best foods to gain weight to fuel their journeys. In contrast, young birds gain weight more slowly and may not always feed most efficiently as they prepare to migrate.

Adult birds have learned the importance of arriving to breeding grounds or winter ranges earlier in order to attract the best mates, defend the safest territories and secure the richest food resources. Young birds do not yet have this experience, and are thus in less of a hurry to begin their monumental travels. Once the journey is underway, mature birds will already be familiar with the migration route and may streamline their travels to cover less overall distance, while young birds are apt to wander more widely. An adult bird also has more experience in dealing with wind gusts, bad storms and other unexpected weather conditions that may disorient younger birds.

Mortality is high among migrating birds, particularly juveniles, but those that are strongest and most adaptable will complete their journeys successfully, returning to their breeding grounds each spring to raise a new brood that they'll leave behind when migration begins.

MORE REASONS TO MIGRATE

Just as migration is more complex than a simple journey, so too are the reasons behind it. Beyond food abundance and breeding necessity, other factors can also influence why birds migrate, including:

CLIMATE

Birds have evolved different layers of plumage to survive in different habitats. Many northern birds would stifle in tropical summers, but are well equipped to enjoy cooler northern seasons as they raise their families. Similarly, cooler northern areas are gentler on delicate chicks as they first hatch and grow. But as temperatures drop below tolerable levels, even these hardier species need to migrate to avoid the harshest winter climates.

PREDATORS

Just as tropical regions have a greater diversity of birds, they also have a greater diversity of predators looking to make an easy meal of eggs and chicks. By migrating to more isolated areas, birds can avoid the crush of predators threatening their vulnerable young, and therefore increase their chances of a productive breeding season. Some birds even opt to breed in very remote locations, such as rocky cliffs or isolated islands, to minimize predation risks.

Though indirectly, these minor factors behind bird migrations still support these movements as necessary for food resources and breeding survival.

COMMON EMU ♂♀
(Dromaius novaehollandiae)

TYPE OF MIGRATION:
Nomadic, Seasonal, Latitudinal

While migrations are often thought of as astonishing feats of flight, not all migratory birds use their wings for propulsion. The common emu undertakes the longest bird migration for a flightless species, walking as far as 500 kilometres (310 miles) to find the best food and water sources throughout Australia, travelling up to 25 kilometres (15 miles) a day. They travel in pairs or may form small groups, generally migrating during daylight hours as they forage. Their long walks are especially important because emu droppings disperse seeds and thus help replant habitat and increase plant diversity. During winter, common emus in western regions of Australia tend to travel south, while during summer they're more likely to head north. Eastern populations, however, are much more erratic wanderers. Overall, the common emu's directions, routes and migration distances are highly variable, largely depending on seasonal rains and where food is most plentiful.

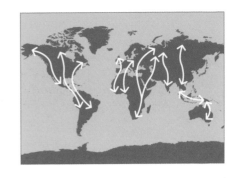

OSPREY ♂♀
(Pandion haliaetus)

TYPE OF MIGRATION:
Seasonal, Latitudinal, Nomadic

The osprey is the most widespread, cosmopolitan raptor in the world, and it breeds or migrates on every continent except Antarctica, from Scandinavia to Africa, from Alaska to South America and from Mongolia to India. Its long, boldly marked wings with splayed 'fingers' are easy to identify in flight, making it a favourite for birders of all experience levels to see. The osprey's migration isn't entirely simple, however, and careful observation reveals that in autumn, mature females start their journeys first, followed by males, then lastly by young ospreys embarking on their first long trips.

Because of their inexperience, juvenile ospreys tend to wander more and may backtrack or follow meandering routes, while adult ospreys migrate along more direct paths. In the spring, on the other hand, males migrate earlier than females in order to secure their territories and attract mates as they arrive. In areas where ospreys are seen year-round, such as Japan, Indonesia and Australia, these birds can still be somewhat nomadic, moving around to seek out the best food sources. Ospreys are solitary migrants and travel alone, generally taking 30–45 days to complete their journeys.

TYPES OF BIRD MIGRATION

While everyone, whether or not they consider themselves a birder or birdwatcher, an ornithologist or naturalist, or just a hobbyist or interested observer, can generally agree on what migration is and why birds do it, it's surprisingly difficult to answer some seemingly easy questions about these amazing journeys.

• When does migration occur?
• In what direction does migration move?
• How far do birds migrate?

Ask when migration happens, and 'spring' and 'autumn' are the most common answers. They're also the most incorrect. While the vernal and autumnal equinoxes – the official start dates for spring and autumn – are based on the earth's angle to the sun relative to the equator, birds aren't astronomers, they don't calculate equatorial planes, and they rarely follow the precise dates of the Gregorian calendar.

In fact, bird migration occurs 365 days a year, every year, with bonus days for extra travel in leap years. Birds that have to travel further between breeding and non-breeding ranges may begin their journeys earlier and reach their final destinations later than other species with shorter routes. And regardless of calendar dates, anyone living in Alaska, Norway or Siberia understands very well that 'spring' and 'autumn' don't always coincide with conventional dates, and that's not to mention the reversal of seasons between the northern and southern hemispheres.

But bird migration is always north–south or east–west, right? Tell that to the budgerigar (*Melopsittacus undulatus*), whose resource-dependent migration may follow local storm systems and abundant rainfall to create a looping, twisty path through the Australian outback. Or ask any of the innumerable vagrant birds who follow crazy routes all their own, such as the purple gallinule (*Porphyrio martinicus*), a brilliantly coloured rail-like bird familiar in North and South America that can occasionally be seen in Iceland, Norway or even Switzerland when its migration goes awry.

Surely distance has to be a key factor in determining migration? After all, a bird flying from a tree to a feeder and back is not migrating. While that's true, it's also true that there is no set distance that a bird must fly to be considered a migrant. The Arctic tern (*Sterna paradisaea*) undertakes an epic pole-to-pole migration that can be over 40,000 kilometres (25,000 miles) there and back – over 70,000 kilometres (40,000 miles) if its wandering path is calculated. At the same time, the Clark's nutcracker (*Nucifraga columbiana*), a sturdy bird of the western North American mountains, may only migrate a few hundred metres to escape the harshest winter weather of the peaks and enjoy a restful getaway in the foothills.

With so much variation, it's difficult to talk in generalities, and what applies to one migratory bird doesn't necessarily apply to another. A birder is just as likely to see a long-distance migrant making its way in early February as they are to see a mid-distance migrant on a circuitous route in July, or a short-distance migrant on the move in November.

To better understand migration, then, it is essential to understand the different types of migration and the birds that make these widely varied voyages. There are a dozen different varieties, and at any given time, birds may be making any of these journeys.

SEASONAL MIGRATION

This is the most common, familiar and predictable
type of bird migration, the one that conforms to the
spring and autumn timeline of migratory movement.
As seasons and resource abundances change, seasonally
migrant birds move between ranges so their survival needs
are better met. The peaks of seasonal migration do indeed
correspond to the general heights of spring and autumn,
as more birds are on the move during these periods.

ALTITUDINAL MIGRATION

Altitudinal or vertical migration has nothing to do with the altitudes at which migrating birds fly, which could be anything from just a few metres to 7.5 kilometres (25,000 feet) or more, and everything to do with birds changing their geographical altitudes in mountain ranges. Many of the hardiest alpine species, those that thrive in breeding ranges above tree lines, drop to lower altitudes to escape the bitter winters of the peaks. While these birds are well equipped for cold weather, moving short distances down the mountain slopes brings them into better cover, milder weather and richer food supplies to last out the winter.

LATITUDINAL MIGRATION

Latitudes are the north/south distances of a migration, and a latitudinal migrant generally follows a north/south or south/north path on its seasonal travels. This orientation is often guided by geographical features, such as coastlines, deserts and mountain ranges, which may inhibit birds from choosing a different direction. This applies to many neotropical migrants in North America and South America, as well as birds in Africa and eastern Asia.

LONGITUDINAL MIGRATION

Ninety degrees apart from latitudinal migration, longitudinal migration follows a general east/west or west/east path. This directional orientation is most common in Europe and northern Africa, where major geographic barriers such as the Mediterranean Sea, the Sahara Desert and the Alps prohibit many birds from migrating great distances north or south.

CLARK'S NUTCRACKER ♂♀
(Nucifraga columbiana)

TYPE OF MIGRATION:
Seasonal, Altitudinal, Irruptive

A migration journey doesn't have to cover a great distance to make a great difference to birds. The Clark's nutcracker only migrates a few hundred yards, but in its harsh alpine habitat, that small change in elevation is essential to survive winter storms and cold snaps. Because this bird's preferred habitat is at the very edge of the tree line in the Rocky Mountains of North America, even a small shift down the slopes during the hardest weeks of winter means better shelter and more accessible food. Some Clark's nutcrackers, however, will move further afield, especially in years when cone seed crops are particularly poor. Vagrant sightings during these irruption years have been recorded as far from the Rocky Mountains as Illinois, Missouri, Texas and Alabama. In gentler winters when seed crops are abundant, these birds may not move at all.

MOULT MIGRATION

Adult birds are at their most vulnerable when they are moulting. The loss of prominent feathers may impair their flight abilities, and in fact many ducks, such as the redhead (*Aythya americana*), are rendered temporarily flightless when they moult. Before shedding their feathers, some birds join a moult migration and relocate to a safer, more secluded area while their plumage regenerates. By migrating in numbers, the birds take advantage of group security until they are able to fend for themselves effectively again, at which time they will disperse.

LOOP MIGRATION

It's a misconception that birds always travel the same direct path back and forth when they migrate. Many birds follow a seasonal loop – a circular path with distinctly different routes in different seasons leading to and from the same end points. The bar-tailed godwit (*Limosa lapponica*), for example, loops from New Zealand to Australia and through eastern Asia to Alaska in the spring, but in the autumn travels directly across the Pacific Ocean and over Hawaii on its way south again. Similarly, the rufous hummingbird (*Selasphorus rufus*) travels north from Mexico to Alaska along the Pacific Coast of North America in the spring when coastal flowers are blooming, but returns south through interior mountain regions in late summer when mountain meadows are in full bloom.

LEAP-FROG MIGRATION

Some migratory birds 'leap-frog' over a core population of their own species that remains in the same area year-round. Northern birds, for example, might pass over a core population en route to more southerly destinations without the different migratory and sedentary groups mixing extensively. In the central populations resources and conditions are suitable for year-round residency, but birds on the fringe migrate to better areas instead. This leap-frog migration has been noted in a number of species, including the dunlin (*Calidris alpina*), golden eagle (*Aquila chrysaetos*) and common hawk-cuckoo (*Hierococcyx varius*).

NOMADIC MIGRATION

This type of migration is less predictable, but still includes seasonal elements as birds move to find the best resources. Nomadic migration is most common in harsh desert environments, where prominent water sources and strong blooms of fruit and flowers may spring up overnight after sudden rainfalls, giving birds and other wildlife the opportunity to breed and safely raise their young while the abundance lasts. Birds such as the Australian zebra finch (*Taeniopygia castanotis*), black swan (*Cygnus atratus*) and griffon vulture (*Gyps fulvus*) are all nomadic migrants.

Black Swan *(Cygnus atratus)*

BUDGERIGAR ♂♀
(Melopsittacus undulatus)

TYPE OF MIGRATION:
Nomadic

The most familiar parrot in the world, the budgerigar is typically believed not to migrate at all, but that isn't strictly the case. While these small, colourful birds do stay in the same general range year-round, they aren't always in the same spots within that broad range. Instead, they wander throughout Australia, following seasonal rains and the resources those rains bring, including fresh water and the grass seeds that appear quickly when moisture arrives.

Wherever and whenever food and water are abundant, budgerigars will breed, and they have to nomadically migrate to follow that abundance. Budgerigars may travel up to 400 kilometres (250 miles) in one day and follow storm clouds using their keen eyesight. In especially wet years, however, they may not migrate much at all. When not breeding, they stay in smaller groups, but where conditions are favourable, tremendous flocks can form, numbering as many as 10,000 budgies or more.

IRRUPTIVE MIGRATION

Even more unpredictable is irruptive migration. Whereas nomadic migration still has some seasonal regularity related to weather patterns, bird irruptions do not always occur every year, but nevertheless remain tied to food resources. These mass migrations are most common among birds in Arctic regions, and may occur either when the breeding season is such a success that the population swells and birds have to venture further than normal to find sufficient food, or when local food stocks crash and birds need to migrate to find adequate resources. In either case, it is food availability that drives irruptive migration. Any type of food fluctuation can trigger an irruption, from a drop in the cone crops that feed the two-barred crossbill (*Loxia leucoptera*) to a fall in the prey populations that feed the snowy owl (*Bubo scandiacus*).

DRIFT MIGRATION

Typically not considered a 'true' type of migration because it lacks any predictability or guaranteed seasonal recurrence, drift migration is when large groups of migrating birds 'drift' from their expected course to end up in a location outside their typical route. This can happen, for example, when a heavy storm blows migrating birds travelling from Scandinavia to Poland or Germany westward to the United Kingdom. Tremendous fallout events can occur as a result of drift migration as exhausted, storm-swept birds concentrate on coasts and other edge habitats to rest and refuel. This type of migration is more common in autumn when inexperienced birds are travelling and get more easily caught up in unfamiliar wind patterns.

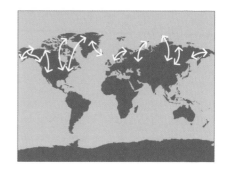

SNOWY OWL ♀
(Bubo scandiacus)

TYPE OF MIGRATION:
Seasonal, Irruptive

One of the most spectacular owls, the snowy owl is an almost impossible spot for many birders because of its high northern tundra range. These owls do migrate short distances in winter, heading slightly south from their circumpolar distribution to seek out more prey when ice and snow blanket their breeding range. When prey is abundant, however, they are less likely to move. In years of severe prey shortage snowy owls make spectacular irruptions that can bring them hundreds of kilometres further south than expected. These irruptions are irregular and difficult to predict, but in more dramatic years, snowy owls have been recorded as far south as Bermuda, Florida, Hawaii, central France and the Azores. Such irruptions are geographically irregular as well, and if snowy owls are irruptive one year in one location, they do not necessarily make outstanding movements throughout their entire range in the same year.

DISPERSAL MIGRATION

Another debated type of migration, dispersal is a one-time journey undertaken by younger birds. It occurs when these birds are chased out of their parents' year-round territory as they reach maturity and have to seek their own space. When these youngsters are on the move they can appear in unexpected locations, triggering some wonderful bird sightings. While dispersal migration only occurs once in an individual bird's lifetime rather than being an annual event, it still has the seasonal predictability and recurrence that helps define migration as a whole.

REVERSE MIGRATION

A reverse migration is one that goes in the opposite direction than expected, such as when a bird that would normally fly south for winter heads determinedly north instead. These are mistakes, and birds on reverse migrations often end up as vagrants far from their typical ranges. While this type of accidental migration is not yet well understood, it is believed to be an aberration among individual birds, perhaps caused by their navigation senses being inadvertently reversed and leading them the wrong way. It is most common among juvenile birds inexperienced in migrating, and can present exciting opportunities for birders to see unexpected species, such as a roseate spoonbill (*Platalea ajaja*) close to the Canadian border rather than in its Mexican winter range.

It is rare that any one bird uses just one form of migration. A longitudinal migrant may also travel in a seasonal loop, during which it could be caught up in a drift migration. Alternatively, half of its migration may be more latitudinal than longitudinal. In a bad year that same bird might be part of an irruptive migration, or one of its offspring could become a reverse migrant the next year, appearing as a vagrant far from known locations and triggering great excitement among birders.

PREPARING FOR MIGRATION

No matter what type of migration birds undertake, how far they travel, or why they make their journey, there are certain preparations that can help make their travels a success. Just as a marathon runner trains before a race, birds have evolved to prepare themselves for migration by undergoing different physiological and behavioural changes that help improve their chances of a successful trip. These changes are triggered by fluctuating light levels as the seasons shift and the time for migration draws near.

Moulting is often the first step in preparing for the long migration flight. Fresh feathers fit together more smoothly for better aerodynamics, which means more efficient energy use when flying. This not only helps birds travel greater distances while using less fuel, but also gives them better manoeuvrability in the air to take advantage of the best wind currents, avoid obstacles and dodge predators.

But even the most efficient flight won't be enough to help birds migrate successfully if they don't have enough energy to make the trip. Several weeks before travelling, changing sunlight levels trigger hormonal shifts in birds' brains, lowering their satiety indicators and compelling them to overeat. This state of increased appetite is called hyperphagia, and allows birds to gain significant weight before they migrate. A tiny bird such as the blackpoll warbler (*Setophaga striata*), which typically weighs just 12 grams (0.42 ounces), can nearly double its weight leading up to migration. This excess fat will fuel its more than 3,200-kilometre (2,000-mile) journey between Canada and South America, when it may lose as much as 1 percent of its weight during each hour in flight.

To better facilitate weight gain, many birds also experience digestive tract changes before they migrate. The tract may swell, allowing for faster digestion so they can eat more without difficulty. Birds will also change their diets to take in richer food sources that can be better stored as extra fat. As migration approaches, many insectivorous species, such as warblers and flycatchers, will eat greater numbers of aphids, since these insects have a higher sugar content than other invertebrates. Warblers may also sip more sugar-rich nectar. Birds that migrate through olive-producing regions near the Mediterranean, such as the song thrush (*Turdus philomelos*), choose olives with higher levels of unsaturated fats that can be more easily converted to body fat, which is readily metabolized for flight energy.

However, it is equally important that birds don't carry too much weight as they fly. Even while they undergo changes to gain fat, birds lose weight in other areas before their long travels. Their sexual organs often shrink to near nothingness, as these will not be needed during the flight and the weight would only slow the birds down. Just as the birds begin migration, their previously expanded digestive tract, including their gizzard, stomach, intestines and liver, will also shrink again, eliminating that excess weight at a time when the birds will be flying more and feeding less. Some birds even lose mass in their leg muscles prior to migration.

All the extra energy birds store as fat won't be useful during migration if their bodies don't function efficiently, and there are other changes different birds undergo to make the most of every calorie they ingest. The red knot (*Calidris canutus*), for example, increases the size of its heart and pectoral muscles before migration, allowing it to fly more powerfully between its breeding range in

Arctic Tern
(*Sterna paradisaea*)

the high Arctic and its non-breeding range as far away as Argentina and Chile. Other species, such as the bar-tailed godwit (*Limosa lapponica*), increase their red blood cell concentration and the haemoglobin levels within those cells prior to migration, which allows more efficient distribution of oxygen to muscles during the strenuous flight, alleviating soreness and disorientation.

Despite these amazing adaptations, physiological changes alone don't adequately prepare birds for a successful migration. In the days and weeks leading up to the start of their journey, many birds start growing restless and anxious, a condition known as *Zugunruhe*, German for movement or migration (*Zug*) and restlessness or anxiety (*Unruhe*). This migratory restlessness has been observed in caged birds prevented from migrating, as well as in the staging flocks of wild birds that make short practice flights before leaving properly on their travels. The fluttering of wings, hopping about and short preparatory flights all help strengthen wing muscles and sharpen senses before birds set off on longer, more challenging journeys.

Exactly which changes an individual bird experiences physically and to its daily feeding and exercise activities vary according to the type of migration it undertakes and route it follows. Birds with shorter, less intensive migrations tend to make fewer changes, while birds with longer, more stressful journeys adapt more extensively.

GREET SNIPE ♂♀
(Gallinago media)

TYPE OF MIGRATION:
Seasonal, Latitudinal

Most snipes are reclusive and hard to see, but the great snipe is a celebrity in the birding world for its record-breaking migration. These chubby avians migrate from Scandinavia and Siberia to sub-Saharan Africa in as little as 48 hours, flying at speeds of up to 97 kilometres per hour (60 miles per hour). While other birds do fly faster, several factors make the great snipe's flight particularly extraordinary. First, these birds don't have the most aerodynamic wing shape, with relatively blunt wings rather than

streamlined pointed wingtips. Second, they're generally not assisted by the wind – their speed is pure powered flight rather than the result of helpful tailwinds. What's more, great snipes undertake their southbound autumn migration without stopping – though in spring they tend to migrate more casually, making several rest stops along the way. Ornithologists are continually studying great snipes to learn more about just how these birds manage such remarkable migration feats.

MIGRATION ROUTES

Picture a map of bird migrations and it's likely to consist of a variety of popular flyways: distinct corridors that mark the main routes followed by birds between dedicated breeding and non-breeding ranges. The problem with flyways, however, is that they don't exist – at least not in the way a map represents them. Even the start and end points of a bird's migration, their different seasonal ranges, aren't as clear-cut as GPS coordinates or field-guide outlines, and birds certainly pay no attention to national borders or political boundaries.

It's true that birds tend to populate areas that meet their survival needs, and these ranges can generally be described according to geography. Similarly, different geographic barriers – mountain ranges, rift valleys, expansive deserts, large bodies of water, glaciers and so on – do create formidable obstacles to migration. Migrating birds often fly around those obstacles, choosing the easiest routes that will allow them to conserve energy and reach their destinations on time and in good health. Together, these facts can make it seem as though birds are only flying from precise areas along specific routes, with relatively empty, bird-free regions between the major flyways.

But this perception isn't true. Birds migrate on and over every square kilometre of land within and between their general seasonal ranges. Small changes, such as a quick storm, a riverbed transformed during an earlier flood, or a burnt area from a wildfire, can easily alter the exact route migrating birds follow. Hurricanes can change coastlines, avalanches can alter land contours, and even earthquakes can shift the best feeding areas, causing birds to move their ranges and routes away from previously determined

sites and perceived flyways. Air currents, wind patterns and seasonal weather systems can also affect the precise routes birds fly during migration.

Still, the basic idea of flyways is a sound one, and there are more heavily travelled routes followed by greater numbers of migrating birds. Every continent includes several of these preferred migration pathways – routes where wind currents, geographical landforms and survival resources are all at their best to support birds' movements. Along those routes are key destinations beloved by birders as well – hot spots where tired birds often congregate in outrageous numbers that provide excellent viewing and photography opportunities.

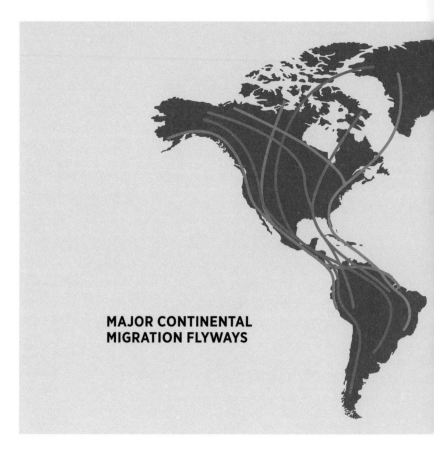

MAJOR CONTINENTAL MIGRATION FLYWAYS

These hot spots or 'migrant traps' are often at the edge of habitat changes, such as the first offshore island or coastal wetland encountered after open sea, or a forest or jungle fringe adjacent to an unforgiving desert. In these key spots, birds can rest and refuel either after they've crossed the obstacle or before they tackle it.

In very few areas extreme geography creates even narrower travel routes, leading to ridiculously inflated congregations of migratory birds. At these bottlenecks,

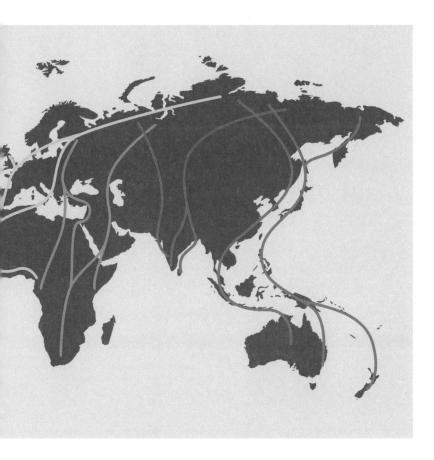

birders can experience sightings and numbers that seem
like pure fiction. In a single day it might be possible to
see more than a dozen different species of raptor – eagles,
vultures, kites, hawks and others – numbering not in the
tens of thousands, or hundreds of thousands, but literally
millions of birds. Migration bottlenecks in Veracruz,
Mexico; Panama City, Panama; and Eilat, Israel are
among the best sites to witness such spectacles.

SWIFT PARROT ♂♀
(Lathamus discolor)

TYPE OF MIGRATION:
Seasonal, Latitudinal, Nomadic

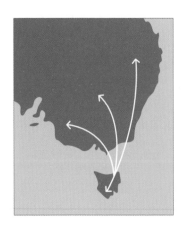

One of the few truly migratory parrots in the world, the critically endangered swift parrot moves from eastern Tasmania to southeastern Australia, heading north in the autumn and south in the spring. Before migrating they gather in flocks of up to 500 birds, but smaller groups of just 10–20 birds are more common, particularly as they cross the 240-kilometre (150-mile) wide Bass Strait separating Tasmania and Australia. Once in their winter range they continue to be somewhat nomadic in order to seek out the best food resources, especially flowering trees rich in nectar. Their streamlined bodies are ideal for swift, agile flight, and the up to 2,000-kilometre (1,200-mile) journey they make between their breeding and wintering ranges is the longest migration of any parrot species, even before their winter wanderings begin.

TO FLOCK OR NOT TO FLOCK

Just because birds are migrating in tremendous numbers along the same route and in close proximity to one another, it doesn't necessarily mean they're migrating in a flock.

Those birds that are highly social throughout the year, especially those that nest in dense colonies, do migrate as dedicated flocks of up to hundreds or thousands of individual birds. Some of the most notable and largest migratory flocks are formed by waterfowl such as ducks, geese and swans, as well as social birds such as cranes, pelicans, waxwings, flamingos, swifts, swallows and shorebirds.

Migrating in a flock has many benefits for individual birds beyond just social or familial companionship. With more birds in the flock, there are more eyes to watch for predators, and more potential targets if a hunter does attack, helping ensure at least some of the group are safe. Similarly, travelling in greater numbers can also mean better success in spotting shelter and food sources during the journey.

Goldcrest
(*Regulus regulus*)

Bird flocks flying in V- or J-shaped formations, called echelons, conserve energy by taking advantage of individual slipstream patterns, much like race cars draft one another to reduce drag and save fuel. Echelons may contain just a few birds or can comprise many dozens of birds flying together, either in one long echelon or in several smaller groups that make up a larger overall flock. Depending on the species, flight formation and air conditions, birds can save as much as 10–20 percent of their energy when flying in a coordinated flock, and even travel at faster speeds than solo fliers under similar conditions.

Travelling in a flock may also improve navigation, allowing birds to work together to choose a route. If one or two individuals have poor navigation senses or are less experienced at migrating, they can rely on the more acute overall directions of the group to find their way.

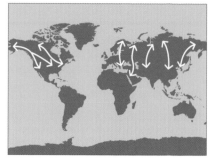

BOHEMIAN WAXWING ♂♀
(Bombycilla garrulus)

TYPE OF MIGRATION:
Seasonal, Irruptive, Latitudinal

The most widespread of the three waxwing species, the bohemian waxwing is a circumpolar bird found in Russia, Scandinavia, Asia and North America, but it doesn't stay in its typical Arctic range every year. Bohemian waxwings have strong, irregular migrations that may send flocks of hundreds of birds roaming far south of their regular range to satisfy their berry-loving appetites when northern-forest crops are poor. One bohemian waxwing can eat 600–1,000 berries during a single winter day, and because they travel in such large flocks, these birds can easily strip a location of food quickly and will continue moving on to the next available feast. On rare occasions, bohemian waxwings have been recorded in locations as far south as Texas, Arizona, Bermuda, Spain, Turkey and Taiwan.

Flocks don't have to be huge to have major benefits for birds. Many species that do not gather in big flocks throughout the year, but are nevertheless generally social, will flock together while migrating. The European bee-eater (*Merops apiaster*), for example, stays in small groups of five to 40 individuals all year long, including during migration as it makes its 14,000-kilometre (8,700-mile) journey between its breeding range in Europe and its non-breeding range in sub-Saharan Africa.

Despite the benefits that group travel may provide to migrating birds, the hugest, most impressive-looking flocks may not really be flocks at all. Hundreds, thousands and even millions of raptors appear to migrate simultaneously over the Isthmus of Panama, with elegantly coordinated flight paths and even surprisingly synchronous wing beats. Yet these solitary birds are not migrating together and have no interaction as individuals. As the geography of the connection between North and South America 'funnels' migrating birds into a perceived flyway path, it also creates the illusion of a flock among less social species.

In this case, individually migrating birds of prey are simply taking advantage of the same air currents and wind patterns, along with other essential resources, in order to fly more easily and efficiently. Raptors typically migrate during the day once thermal currents have warmed sufficiently to ease their soaring flight. Because these birds use such thermals almost exclusively, they need to migrate over land where the air is warmest and rises properly to enable their flight pattern. When so many birds have just one narrow strip of land to pass over between their breeding and non-breeding ranges, it can easily appear as if they're migrating together. It's just like cars on a highway – individual drivers may be following the same traffic laws on the road, crossing the same bridges over a river, and using the same exits on the other side to reach their destinations, but they are not travelling together.

Still, although the flock is only an illusion, impressive numbers of raptors migrating at the same time and in the same place can make for a stunning spectacle. In Veracruz, Mexico, for example, where the Atlantic Ocean to the east and the Sierra Madre mountains to the west funnel migrating raptors into a very narrow corridor, more than 4.5 million birds of prey will pass a single point during migration season. In one day, counts of more than 100,000 raptors have been recorded at watch sites in Veracruz – an average of nearly 140 raptors every minute – yet not one of these broad-winged hawks (*Buteo platypterus*), turkey vultures (*Cathartes aura*), Mississippi kites (*Ictinia mississippiensis*) or Swainson's hawks (*Buteo swainsoni*) is part of a coordinated flock.

Mistle Thrush
(*Turdus viscivorus*)

WHAT DO YOU CALL A FLOCK OF RAPTORS?

While migrating groups of raptors are not truly coordinated flocks, seeing a mass of these birds soaring together as they take advantage of the best flight conditions is nonetheless an impressive sight. So impressive, in fact, that many special names are given to flocks of raptors, depending on the species.

Any group of raptors – on the ground or in the air – can be called a 'cast', while a flock of raptors in flight is often called a 'cauldron', 'kettle' or 'boil'. These creative names evoke the image of the roiling, bubbling surface of cooking liquid, which the swirling motions of dozens or hundreds of raptors soaring on the same thermal currents in one small area can often resemble. Other fun names for groups of specific raptors include:

- **Buzzards and vultures:** committee, venue, volt, wake
- **Eagles:** convocation, congregation, jubilee
- **Falcons and hobbies:** ringing, tower
- **Harriers:** harassment, swarm
- **Kestrels:** hover, soar

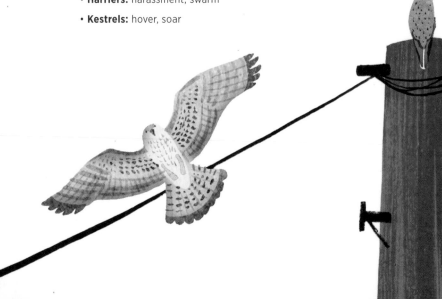

- **Kites:** string
- **Merlins:** illusion
- **Owls:** parliament, wisdom, study, bazaar, glaring

Many flock names come from our perceptions of certain birds. Describing a flock of vultures as a 'wake' conjures images of funerals and, with them, the carcasses these birds feed on. Other names describe how birds tend to fly – kestrels 'hover' while hunting prey – while others relate to the cultural symbolism surrounding a type of bird – owls are perceived as intelligent, hence a 'wisdom' or 'study'. Some flock names are just fun: a 'string' of kites, for instance, evokes the whimsical image of a toy-kite string, while an 'illusion' of merlins is a reference to Merlin the legendary wizard.

As well as raptors such as hawks, vultures and kites, many other birds are solitary migrants taking on tremendous migration journeys with just their own two wings, despite illusions to the contrary. During autumn migration, for example, hummingbirds that might have been very aggressive and territorial just a few weeks earlier will more easily share prime flowerbeds or dedicated feeding stations while travelling. This is the result of the physiological change that these birds undergo just prior to autumn migration. As their sexual organs shrink to reduce their weight, the birds' hormone levels also drop, reducing their territoriality and making them slightly more sociable. This doesn't compel them to migrate in deliberate flocks, but it does help them become more tolerant of other hummingbirds in close proximity and focus on refuelling for further travel rather than defending territories or enticing mates. As in the case of migrating raptors following narrow air currents, hummingbirds feeding en masse can create the illusion of flocking behaviour.

Rails, cuckoos, kingfishers, orioles, woodpeckers, wrens, creepers, kinglets, herons and other birds that are notorious loners at most times of the year also tend to migrate alone. However, even with slightly more congenial personalities that lack the competitiveness found during mating season, these birds still maintain some personal space and relative distance from one another as they migrate and are generally unlikely to be found in large flocks.

Common Kingfisher
(*Alcedo atthis*)

HOW DO HUMMINGBIRDS MIGRATE?

Migration is an amazing feat, and all the more so in the case of the tiniest of birds. Hummingbirds can be as small as just 3 grams (0.1 ounces) and 7–10 centimetres (3–4 inches) in length, yet a number of these birds migrate tremendous distances between their seasonal ranges. The ruby-throated hummingbird (*Archilochus colubris*), for example, migrates nonstop over the Gulf of Mexico, a journey that can stretch anywhere between 800 and 1,500 kilometres (500 and 930 miles), depending on an individual bird's start and end points. So, just how do these tiny birds travel so far?

For many years, it was believed that hummingbirds – and other small songbirds – were incapable of completing these strenuous flights on their own. Instead, they were thought to hitchhike on the backs of stronger birds with better endurance. Today, that migration myth has been thoroughly debunked, and we know a great deal about how hummingbirds migrate.

Ruby-Throated Hummingbird
(*Archilochus colubris*)

Hummingbirds are solo travellers.
These small birds travel alone during migration. A single tiny target is much less noticeable to potential predators, giving hummingbirds better security as they migrate.

Hummingbirds migrate during the day.
Hummingbirds travel from mid-morning to the early evening hours, when the air is warmer and easier for them to maintain the best body temperature.

Hummingbirds fly at low altitudes.
Lower air is denser, making it easier for hummingbirds to manoeuvre. Over land, they typically fly just above the treetops at 6–15 metres (20–50 feet). Over water, they may skim the waves.

Hummingbirds travel as flowers bloom.
Hummingbirds adjust their migratory times and routes to coincide with the most prodigious blooming of nectar-rich flowers, ensuring an ample fuel supply en route.

With all their adaptations, hummingbirds manage to travel 32–40 kilometres (20–25 miles) over land on a typical migration day. That's the equivalent of a 4.6-metre (15-foot) mid-sized car covering more than 1,600 kilometres (1,000 miles) in the same time period!

RUFOUS HUMMINGBIRD ♂
(Selasphorus rufus)

TYPE OF MIGRATION:
Loop, Seasonal, Latitudinal

A colourful and aggressive hummingbird, the rufous hummingbird stands out as much for its migration as for its bright orange plumage and domineering attitude. These tiny birds, weighing just 3.3 grams (0.12 ounces), have the longest migration of any hummingbird, travelling from their northernmost breeding grounds in southeastern Alaska and northwestern Canada to spend the winter in central Mexico, a one-way trip of nearly 6,400 kilometres (4,000 miles). To ensure they have adequate fuel to sustain them, their journey follows a very specific clockwise route. In spring, rufous hummingbirds migrate along the Pacific Coast of North America, where the temperate effects of the Pacific Ocean bring spring – and blooming flowers – early. In late summer and early autumn, these hummingbirds are on the move through interior mountain regions, where flowering mountain meadows offer nourishing nectar.

ARE WE THERE YET?

Whether part of a flock or flying solo, once birds set out on their migration journeys, they may spend anything from a few hours to several weeks or even months travelling between destinations. Some birds are marathon travellers and fly nonstop over oceans or deserts without pausing to refuel, while others rest along the way, or may be forced to stop and wait out storms or poor wind patterns.

Because birds that have to cross huge obstacles such as the Sahara Desert, the Himalayas or the Pacific Ocean are unable to stop safely along the way, they have adapted to tackle those high-endurance flights. The bar-headed goose (*Anser indicus*), for example, migrates over the Himalayas at more than 10,000 metres (33,000 feet) above sea level – the highest-recorded altitude of any bird migration. To survive the very cold, thin air at these heights, the geese have evolved more efficient lungs to fuel their powerful muscles, and more enriched haemoglobin in their blood to ensure they have as much oxygen as they need to complete this fantastic flight.

Just as human travellers have flight layovers or pause at roadside rest points on long car journeys, most birds also make regular stops on their travels. Birds tend to stop off in rich habitats where they can not only rest, but also have plentiful food to refuel for the next leg of their trip. These areas where large numbers of diverse migrating birds stop to take advantage of resources are commonly known as stopover habitats, passage habitats or migrant traps.

The main types of stopover habitat include:

AGRICULTURAL FIELDS

Broad expanses of pastures and agricultural fields
are always helpful for migrating birds, but they are
particularly popular habitats in autumn after the harvest.
At that time, spilled grain or leftover seeds can easily
nourish hungry feathered travellers. In some areas,
farmers flood their fields after harvest or, in spring, fields
may become inundated with rain or melting snow, thus
providing rich temporary wetlands for migrating ducks,
geese and wading birds.

URBAN PARKS

With habitat loss continuing to affect birds, an urban
park – or other city green space such as a riverside walk,
large athletics complex or hidden nature reserve – can be
a haven for tired migrating birds. Many parks may not
only offer mature trees and plants that the surrounding
area sorely lacks, but also ponds and other water features
that will host urban and feral waterfowl alongside
occasional passing migrants.

CEMETERIES

Similar to urban parks, cemeteries can be handy refuges
for migrating birds in areas where other suitable habitat
has become scarce. Because cemeteries often contain
mature trees and are relatively quiet and undisturbed,
birds can often find as much peace and rest there as the
dearly departed.

ISLANDS AND ARCHIPELAGOS

A richly vegetated island can be a welcome oasis for birds migrating across broad areas of water that otherwise offer no opportunities to rest. Because many of these islands remain isolated and fairly unspoilt even today, they make prime habitats for hungry, tired birds. Similarly, a barrier island can also be an ideal stopover habitat for migrating birds before or after they cross a body of water.

PENINSULAS

Because peninsulas jut out into large bodies of water, they can offer migrating birds an extra boost before they begin their perilous crossing, helping make the journey slightly shorter. On return flights, a peninsula represents an early recovery zone for tired birds ahead of the main coastline.

COASTS AND SHORELINES

These habitats border larger bodies of water, such as oceans, broad bays or large lakes, and represent a bird's last opportunity to rest and fuel up before crossing the expanse. For exhausted birds arriving from the opposite direction, these areas provide the first opportunity to recover from the strenuous crossing.

ORCHARDS AND VINEYARDS

During both the spring and autumn migrations, orchards and vineyards can be ideal stopover habitats. In spring, these fields are often in full bloom and, depending on the type of plants being grown, birds might be able to sip the nectar. Even if the plants don't produce nectar, the insects attracted to the blooms will provide a rich protein source for migratory birds. Many birds will also feast on swollen buds and tender new plant growth. In the autumn, ripe fruits are available to bolster energy reserves.

Stopover habitats allow birds to find essentials such as safe shelter, rich food sources and fresh water quickly. This can make the difference between successfully completing a long migration or collapsing from exhaustion or starvation before reaching a safe destination.

Depending on the type of bird and its restoration needs, the local climate, the length of an individual bird's journey, and the time of year, a bird may spend anything from just a few hours to several days or even weeks recuperating at a stopover site. If a bird is migrating late in the season, it may only stay a brief time, particularly in spring when earlier migrants have better success at claiming the best territories and attracting the

strongest mates. On the other hand, a strong storm or passing front might keep birds at the stopover site until flight conditions improve. In autumn, mild weather and rich harvests could encourage birds to stay at a stopover habitat longer. If there are early frosts or approaching storms, migrating birds are likely to continue on their journeys more quickly.

The amount of stops a bird makes along its route also varies. Research that has tracked migrants with different journey lengths has shown that birds are more likely to make just three or four longer stops rather than a series of frequent shorter stops. However, the same factors that affect how long a bird stays at a particular site can also impact the frequency of stops and the lengths of flights between each rest.

Because healthy, thriving stopover habitats can attract a wide variety of species, they can be hot spots for birdwatchers, too. During peak migration periods, the birds at different sites can change daily, and because they are busy refuelling to continue their journeys, they are typically bolder and more easily observed. Many nature centres, birding organizations and conservation groups arrange festivals and other events at such sites during peak migration periods to highlight not only bird migration, but also the incredible value of stopover habitats and how important they are for both resident and travelling birds.

BAR-TAILED GODWIT ♂♀
(Limosa lapponica)

TYPE OF MIGRATION:
Seasonal, Loop, Latitudinal

Travelling to far-flung destinations is a regular habit for the bar-tailed godwit. While its annual migration in its European, African and Asian range is no more or less extraordinary than that of many other birds, the journey undertaken by its North American population is nothing short of outstanding. These bar-tailed godwits migrate from Alaska to New Zealand in one nonstop flight over the Pacific Ocean each autumn, making the roughly 11,000-kilometre (6,800-mile) journey in eight days – the longest nonstop migration of any bird in the world. In spring, however, bar-tailed godwits return along the Asian coast and stop much more frequently, allowing them to arrive at their breeding grounds in peak condition for the rigours of reproduction.

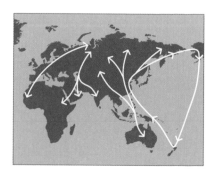

THE NAVIGATION
OF MIGRATION

Why birds migrate, how they prepare for the journey,
the groups they may or may not travel in, where they go,
how often they stop to rest – all these questions can be
answered. But one of the trickier aspects of bird migration
to understand is how all these parts come together to
take birds from point A to point B. When we humans
travel we use GPS, road maps, directional signs, satellite
data, traffic alerts and ask directions to find our way.
But birds have none of these. Instead, they have to rely
on their own unique navigational abilities to steer them
through migration.

MAGNETIC SENSING
Birds are able to orient themselves to the earth's magnetic
field as a result of specialized chemicals and compounds
in their eyes, bills and brains. While this mechanism isn't
yet well understood, studies in 2018 analyzed specialized
proteins called cryptochromes in birds' eyes using Timor
zebra finches (*Taeniopygia guttata*) and European robins
(*Erithacus rubecula*). Unlike many ocular proteins that
fluctuate at different times of day based on light levels,
the Cry4 cryptochrome protein increased during migration
season and did not adjust throughout the day, indicating
that it is used at all times, regardless of light. This could
mean that birds are 'seeing' the earth's magnetic field,
which could give them a highly accurate directional
orientation for migrating.

Similarly, a 2004 study of common reed-warblers
(*Acrocephalus scirpaceus*) noted significant amounts of
iron minerals, including the iron ore magnetite, in their
bills, and that transmissions from those compounds
were sent to their brains, affecting their internal maps.

This sense of geography is another key component of how birds navigate during migration, but more study is needed to further understand just how birds use these chemical interactions on journeys that span hundreds or thousands of kilometres.

GEOGRAPHIC MAPS

Birds have keen senses, possessing visual acuity and hearing that far surpasses that of humans. This extraordinary sensory perception allows them to create internal geographic maps of their ranges and the migration routes between them. Landforms and shapes, including mountains, islands, rivers, canyons and coasts, can all be part of those maps, particularly for birds that migrate during the day, such as raptors, swifts, swallows, pelicans and hummingbirds. Sounds can also become part of the map, such as the splashing of a flowing river, the rumble of waves crashing on a rocky coast, or the wind blowing through a tall forest. How sounds change with distance, altitude and weather patterns can help birds adjust their migration en route, too.

STAR MAPS

While geographic maps can be useful for birds migrating during daylight hours, nocturnal migrants may make equal use of internal star maps and visible stellar patterns. Just as they helped orient human travellers centuries before GPS or online maps were available, the brightest stars in the night sky can also serve as handy navigational aids for birds. Birds that migrate at night, including warblers, orioles, sparrows, thrushes, cuckoos and buntings, are all likely to use the stars to help find their way. Studies conducted in planetariums, where birds have no landforms, sounds or other clues to orient themselves, have confirmed that even small songbirds can see the stars and will line up according to stellar patterns.

The brightest, closest star of all – the sun – also helps migrating birds, and can provide an orientation point to help them set off in the right direction. But what about on overcast days or nights, when neither the sun nor the stars are easily visible? Once again, birds' keen senses are useful here. Because they can see far into the ultraviolet (UV) spectrum, and because up to 80 percent of UV light still penetrates the clouds (depending on depth of cover), birds can use these navigational clues even when the stars aren't visible to human navigators.

LEARNED ROUTES

Just as we can learn directions from other people, some birds can learn migration routes from other, more experienced individuals. In bird species where the juveniles stay with the family group until they mature, young birds commonly learn migration routes from their parents. Sandhill cranes (*Antigone canadensis*), whooping cranes (*Grus americana*) and northern bald ibises (*Geronticus eremita*) are just a few of the species that migrate as families, passing along route information with every trip.

Ultimately, one type of navigation alone isn't likely to get many migratory birds safely to the end of their seasonal journeys, but birds adapt their techniques depending on conditions along the way. While they might get directional information from magnetic fields, they might reinforce that route with a geographic map. At different points in the journey, sound might play a bigger role in adjusting the route, such as when approaching a noisy, rocky coast or passing an echoey canyon. Ultraviolet light from the sun can also help keep the birds on track, particularly on cloudy days and nights, reinforcing the route they may have learned on their first migration with their parents just a few weeks after they hatched.

DO YOU KNOW YOUR BIRD CONSTELLATIONS?

Many night-migrating birds use the brightest star patterns in the sky to orient their flight and navigate their journeys. Humans have done the same for millennia, relying on stars and constellations to cross tremendous distances when other landmarks or references may be unknown or unavailable. As humans have labelled the constellations, many have been given the names of birds:

Apus – The Bird of Paradise
This bold constellation in the southern hemisphere shows a distinct long tail but has no feet, as it was once believed that birds of paradise were footless.

Aquila – The Eagle
A familiar constellation seen throughout the northern hemisphere and well into the southern hemisphere, Aquila is depicted carrying Zeus's thunderbolts or guarding Eros's arrows.

Columba – The Dove
This peaceful constellation is visible in the southern half of the northern hemisphere as well as throughout the southern hemisphere. Also called Noah's Dove, the bird carries a plant sprig.

Corvus – The Crow or The Raven
Representing Apollo's sacred bird from Greek mythology, this constellation with its spread wings is visible in much of the northern hemisphere and in the whole of the southern hemisphere.

Cygnus – The Swan
The 16th largest of the 88 modern constellations recognized by the International Astronomical Union, this soaring constellation is visible in the whole of the northern hemisphere and the northern half of the southern hemisphere.

Grus – The Crane
This long-necked, long-legged constellation was once called Phoenicopterus, The Flamingo, and is seen in the southern third of the northern hemisphere and the whole of the southern hemisphere.

Pavo – The Peacock
This constellation is visible in the southern third of the northern hemisphere and throughout the southern hemisphere, and was believed to be named after the green peafowl (*Pavo muticus*).

Tucana – The Toucan
This southern hemisphere constellation is also visible in the southern quarter of the northern hemisphere, and depicts the plump body and large bill typical of toucans.

DAYTIME OR NIGHTTIME –
WHICH IS BEST FOR MIGRATION?

Which techniques birds use to navigate during migration can largely depend on whether they migrate by day or night. Star maps, for example, aren't as useful to birds that migrate during daylight hours, while visual geographic maps don't help so much at night when landform details can't be seen as accurately. How birds fly and what foods they eat also influence what times are best for them to travel.

Night migration offers birds several benefits, including the ability to avoid night-hunting predators on the ground, as well as raptors that hunt during the day, when warmer air makes raptor migration easier. What's more, cooler night air is less turbulent, allowing small birds to fly more smoothly while expending less energy, helping them go further on the same amount of fuel. Birds that migrate during the day, on the other hand, can take advantage of warmer air currents such as thermals, which allow birds to more easily migrate over mountains. Birds that forage for insects in flight, such as swallows and swifts, also migrate during daylight hours when insects are active and the birds can feed as they fly.

EURASIAN SCOPS-OWL ♂♀
(Otus scops)

TYPE OF MIGRATION:
Seasonal, Latitudinal

While most owls do not migrate, the Eurasian scops-owl, also called the common scops-owl, is an exception, a seasonal migrant that regularly travels between its breeding grounds in Europe and its wintering grounds in sub-Saharan Africa. While a few of these small owls do stay in the southern part of their European range year-round, the vast majority make the journey across the Mediterranean Sea and the Sahara Desert, migrating in small groups at night and roosting during the day. Depending on where an individual

starts and ends its journey, it may begin migrating south in the autumn as early as August, though birds with less distance to travel may not be on their way until November. In spring, owls with greater distances to travel set out in March, while those with shorter routes migrate mostly in April. In both seasons, these owls prefer open country with scattered trees, and may even be seen in gardens and suburban areas.

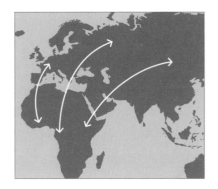

GETTING LOST ALONG THE WAY

Despite all birds' navigational techniques and the stopover habitats that nourish them along the way, migration is not straightforward. Many birds get lost as they travel, ending up hundreds or even thousands of kilometres away from their expected routes and ranges. These vagrant, unexpected sightings can be astonishing, but they also raise questions about how birds come to travel so far from their typical destinations.

Why would the common vermilion flycatcher (*Pyrocephalus rubinus*), with a native range stretching from the southwestern United States and Mexico to South America and Argentina, suddenly appear in Nova Scotia? Why would the European robin (*Erithacus rubecula*), native to western Europe, north Africa and the Middle East, fly in the opposite direction of its typical migration and end up in China, South Korea or Japan? Why would the Pacific loon (*Gavia pacifica*), typically found throughout the Arctic from eastern Russia through Canada and southern Alaska to the Baja Peninsula in North America and south to Japan and the Korean Peninsula in Asia, migrate the wrong way to end up in Ireland, Norway or Italy instead?

We humans expect the occasional road closure, cancelled flight, diverted train or missed bus – all delays that are out of our control. But migratory birds are in command of their own routes and propulsion, so how do they get lost and end up so far away?

Just as there are different factors affecting how, when and why birds migrate, there are also a number of factors that can cause them to get lost along the way.

BAD WEATHER

Any form of transport – planes, cruise ships, cross-country buses – can be delayed or diverted by bad weather, and so can migrating birds. Hurricanes and typhoons can easily blow birds off course, carrying them hundreds of kilometres away from their destinations or pushing seabirds far inland. Indeed any strong weather front or aggressive wind shear may nudge birds off their preferred migration routes, causing them to appear in unexpected locations.

INDIVIDUAL WEAKNESS

Just as not all people are equally adept at following directions or operating their GPS, not all birds have the same keen senses or ability to navigate a challenging migration. Illness or physical weakness, caused by poor food sources or injuries, could impair a bird's navigation and push it astray. Genetic mutations can also affect a bird's inner compass and lead it off course.

COMMON CRANE ♂♀
(Grus grus)

TYPE OF MIGRATION:
Seasonal, Latitudinal

The elegant common crane, also known as the Eurasian crane, is a spectacular bird to see, and it's a spectacular migration that brings it into view for many birders. While the species occupies a fractured year-round range in Turkey, the majority of the population is highly migratory, travelling between its broad northern European and Asian breeding range and its more restricted southeast Asian, Indian mountain, northern African and Nile River Valley non-breeding range.

Despite its wide dispersal the common crane migrates along a corridor roughly 100 kilometres (62 miles) wide, using the same narrow, precise route during both its spring and autumn journeys. Yet some birds do stray far from their expected routes and ranges, with vagrant sightings recorded in Canada, Alaska and other parts of the United States, including around the Great Lakes and in the Great Plains.

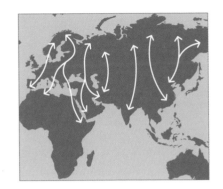

HITCHHIKING

Birds will occasionally hitchhike during migration as they happen upon unusual resting spots. An exhausted bird migrating from Alaska to China, for example, might encounter a strong wind shear and take refuge on a cargo ship in the Pacific Ocean. As the bird rests for a day or two, perhaps enjoying handouts from well-meaning crew members, the ship continues sailing, and the bird might find itself in southern California, Australia or Ecuador instead of its initial destination.

ELECTRONIC INTERFERENCE

While ornithologists and other researchers don't yet know a great deal about how birds navigate using magnetic sensing, it is already clear that electronic interference from stronger and more widespread power lines, mobile-phone towers and wireless signals can disrupt their migration. As the earth's magnetic field becomes more cluttered with artificial signals, birds may not be able to rely on their magnetic sensing as easily, and more will get lost during migration.

LIGHT POLLUTION

Just as changes in the geographic landscape can confuse migrating birds that rely on landforms to find their way, changes in the light landscape can confuse birds that use star maps and patterns to orient themselves. Heavy light pollution around urban areas or commercial developments can block out star patterns completely, causing disoriented birds to crash into obstacles or become exhausted as they struggle to find their way.

CLIMATE CHANGE

An unstable climate means shifting coastlines, rising sea levels, expanding deserts, changing tree lines, and other alterations to geographic landforms that birds rely on for migration navigation. The more the geography changes along a bird's migration route, the more difficult it will be for that bird to successfully migrate following the same route season after season. Eventually it could become irrevocably lost along the way.

Northern Parula
(Setophaga americana)

HABITAT LOSS

Habitat loss affects not only birds' breeding and non-breeding ranges, but also their migration routes. As stopover sites and refuge habitats shift and disappear, a travelling bird will have to seek out new places to rest, which could eventually point it in a different direction from its typical migration. Similarly, changes in coastlines, riverbeds and forest edges as a result of ongoing development, agricultural expansion or natural disasters can alter a bird's mental geographic map and lead it astray.

WHEN LOST BIRDS ARE FOUND AGAIN

When a migrating bird loses its way and ends up far from an expected route or destination, it can be very exciting for birders. Instead of having to travel to see a bird in its native range, they might suddenly be able to see it in their favourite local refuge or in their own backyard. These vagrant birds may stay in the vicinity for several weeks or, if the resources are available to support them, even for the entire season until it is time to migrate again.

Unfortunately, however, many vagrant birds do not survive. A successful migration that leads from a bird's breeding range to its non-breeding range along the shortest route in the shortest time is already challenging, and even then mortality can be high for healthy, strong birds. Birds that get lost often travel further and under more adverse, exhausting conditions. They quickly become worn out and weak, only to find themselves in a completely unfamiliar area alone. At the same time food sources will be unrecognizable, predators unknown, and the stress of the experience can take an even greater toll on the bird's wellbeing.

In rare instances, vagrant birds can be successfully rescued by wildlife rehabilitators who are able to tend to their needs and nurture them back to more robust health. But even then it may not be possible to successfully send the bird on its way, as it will not know how to find its way back home. While it is possible to assist the bird with a ride back to familiar territory, the cost of doing so, as well as regulations about transporting wildlife across international borders, often make such actions prohibitive. Instead, most vagrant birds thrill and delight birders for a few days or weeks before they mysteriously vanish, most likely having succumbed to the elements, unknown predators, or the stresses of their failed journeys.

COMMON POCHARD ♂
(Aythya ferina)

TYPE OF MIGRATION:
Seasonal, Latitudinal, Moult

A widespread diving duck, the common pochard is a large-scale migrant with the majority of its population moving between a northern breeding range in Europe, Russia and central Asia and a southern wintering range in southern Europe, southeastern Asia, India and northern Africa, including further south along the Nile River Valley. They tend to move in large flocks numbering hundreds or thousands of individuals, creating a spectacular sight. Prior to their seasonal migration, limited numbers of male common pochards also practise moult migration, though they don't tend to move far from their breeding grounds at this time. Winter flocks are much larger and more spectacular than summer flocks, which are more spread out to maximize breeding resources. Between their breeding and non-breeding ranges, a central population core in the United Kingdom, France, Germany, Austria, Romania and parts of eastern Turkey and northern Iran is occupied year-round. On rare occasions, vagrant common pochards have been recorded as far afield as the Canary Islands, Guam, the Philippines, Alaska, California and Hawaii.

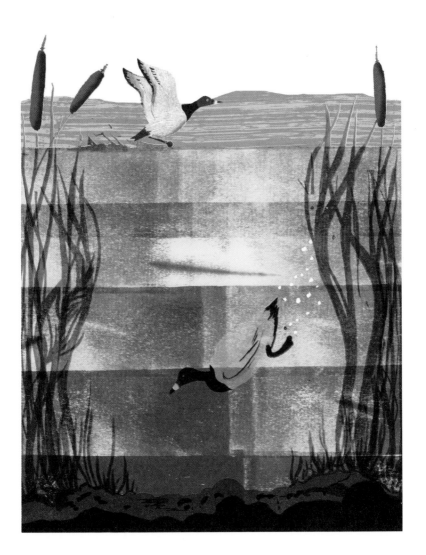

OBSTACLES ON FAMILIAR ROUTES

It isn't just unfamiliar places that make migration so hazardous. Even birds that follow tried-and-tested routes used for generations of feathered travels face many different risks on their journeys.

HABITAT LOSS

One of the greatest and most widespread threats to migratory birds is habitat loss. When habitats – and all the shelter, water and food resources that go with them – are lost, birds can wind up without a destination at one end of their migration or, when losses occur between ranges, a lack of critical stopover sites. Even if birds are thriving at one end of their annual travels, such as in a protected refuge in their breeding range, habitat loss along their migration route or in their non-breeding range can be disastrous. Healthy, robust birds that begin their migration positively may never complete or return from their journey.

EXHAUSTION

With fewer resources available along bird migration routes and habitat loss removing stopover habitats, birds can easily succumb to exhaustion as they migrate. Exhausted birds may simply fall out of the sky as they falter in flight, or if they do manage to land safely, they may be less wary about predators and other nearby risks.

STARVATION

Habitat loss and climate change both impact migrating birds' food supplies, and with less food around, there is greater competition for what resources are available. When birds cannot gain enough excess fat to fuel their migration or are unable to refuel sufficiently along the way, they can easily starve to death as they travel.

COLLISIONS

While birds are well able to avoid mid-air collisions with familiar obstacles such as trees, cliffs and other birds, unfamiliar, unnatural obstacles pose a much greater risk. Windows and reflective glass buildings are the greatest collision hazard for migratory birds, particularly when the surfaces reflect plants and sky and seem to offer the perfect safe haven. Other collision obstacles include wind turbines, power lines, mobile-phone towers and offshore oil rigs, especially in open areas where obstacles are not expected and birds unused to flying around hazards may not be as agile in the air.

PREDATORS

Birds are at risk from hungry predators throughout the year, but the risk is even greater during migration. As birds pass through unfamiliar areas, they may not be as aware of local predators, particularly invasive or introduced species such as feral cats, ferrets and rats. These opportunistic predators will easily prey on tired, hungry birds.

POLLUTION

Different types of contamination, from massive oil spills to overuse of pesticides and fertilizers on suburban lawns and gardens, can dramatically impact bird migration. Pollution can easily damage habitats, and even if the plants remain intact, toxins can destroy food sources, from insect, fish and prey populations to grain, seed and fruit production. Furthermore, it only takes a small speck of pollution directly on a bird – a drop of oil the size of a thumbnail, for example – to disrupt its natural insulation and lead to hypothermia, excessive preening or undue stress, all of which can impair its migration success.

LITTER

Equally threatening to migratory birds are the dangers of litter, such as plastic. This debris not only damages habitats, but if it is accidentally ingested, sharp shards can cause fatal internal injuries to birds. Migratory birds, in particular, are at risk because they may be unfamiliar with food sources in stopover habitats and more likely to nibble at tempting trash. Even if the debris does not cause internal damage, undigestible bits can clog a bird's digestive tract and the bird may starve to death even as it believes it is eating.

NATURAL DISASTERS

Birds are just as at risk from natural disasters as humans. Earthquakes, tsunamis, hurricanes, mudslides, floods and wildfires can destroy habitats and wipe out food sources critical for migrating birds, while early or late blizzards or cold snaps can also disrupt migration and catch both early and late migrants unawares.

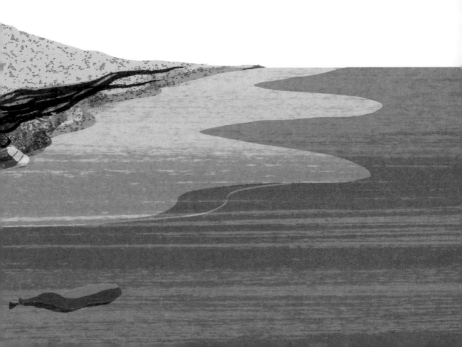

HUNTING

While properly managed hunting that includes population monitoring and licensing efforts is not a severe threat to migratory birds, problems arise when neighbouring areas fail to communicate their hunting guidelines. A bird that may be hunted in one area could be threatened or endangered in another, while excess hunting as birds move between their ranges could have dramatic population impacts. Furthermore, accidental shootings caused by hunters failing to accurately identify migrating birds can also be devastating.

OVERFISHING

Many puffins, albatrosses, pelicans, shearwaters, petrels, penguins and different raptors, including the osprey (*Pandion haliaetus*), rely on healthy fish populations for sufficient prey, particularly as these birds head out to sea after breeding or migrate across oceans. When areas are overfished, not only will these birds have fewer food resources to rely on for migratory refuelling, but they face greater risk of getting caught in irresponsibly left nets or longlines.

POACHING

The most brilliantly coloured migratory birds are at greatest risk from poachers, particularly during spring migration when their plumage is at its most dramatic. These illegal captures may force wild birds into the pet trade, or simply strip them of feather plumes, often with fatal consequences. Poachers also sometimes set traps for migratory birds along perceived flyways or at key stopover sites in order to illegally capture greater numbers of birds for food, sale or trade.

HUMAN IGNORANCE

When little is known about the hazards birds face during migration, it is impossible to mitigate those hazards and help birds migrate more successfully. While many birders are aware of some of the most prominent and obvious bird migration risks, many non-birders have little or no awareness of the obstacles their most common and familiar birds face on their travels. Spreading the word about migration hazards is essential to safeguard all birds, whichever way they may be travelling in whatever season.

Despite so many obstacles and what would seem to be overwhelming odds, billions of birds do successfully migrate every year. However, at the same time, many other birds have evolved to counter those risks by not migrating at all.

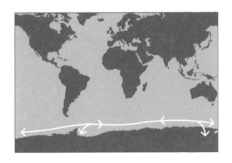

EMPEROR PENGUIN ♂♀
(Aptenodytes forsteri)

TYPE OF MIGRATION:
Seasonal, Dispersal

Not all migratory birds fly, and the emperor penguin makes amazing migrations through the water using its powerful swimming ability. While these wandering birds don't have a definite non-breeding range and spend much of their time at sea following available fish, krill and other food sources, their travels still add up to an impressive journey around the Southern Ocean – up to 4,800 kilometres (3,000 miles) from their nesting sites. Emperor penguins are some of the most impressive swimming birds, able to dive to an average depth of 200 metres (660 feet), with some individuals even recorded at an astonishing 530 metres (1,740 feet). The extent of their land travels, considering their short legs and shuffling gait, is only slightly less impressive, with emperor penguins migrating up to 95–160 kilometres (60–100 miles) inland to their breeding colonies. Furthermore, shifting and melting ice means they never take exactly the same route to and from the ocean.

FORGET IT, I'M NOT GOING

Given the tremendous effort necessary for migration and all the risks birds face along the way, it's not surprising that a great number of birds don't migrate at all. While the migratory habits of all the world's more than 10,000 bird species are not well documented, and different organizations may classify migration differently based on a variety of factors, as many as 25–60 percent of bird species may not make significant long-distance migrations. However, many of these birds may still be nomadic or have more limited migratory patterns.

Instead of expending energy on risky, long journeys, non-migrating birds have adapted their energy for year-round living in the same space. This affords them significant advantages over their travelling cousins, including being able to keep the same familiar territory throughout the year and having more time to care for growing chicks or raise multiple broods instead of making long journeys. In order to use these advantages, however, non-migratory birds typically:

HAVE MORE ADAPTABLE DIETS.
Rather than relying on the same food sources throughout the year, birds that don't migrate will often shift their feeding habits depending on what foods are more abundant at different times of year. In spring when plants are blooming and insect populations are rising, these birds will dine primarily on flowers, nectar or insects. In autumn, however, seeds, berries, and nuts may make up a greater part of their diet. Migratory birds on the other hand, often eat the same types of foods year-round, and their travels take them to where those foods are more plentiful in different seasons.

JOIN MIXED FLOCKS IN THE NON-BREEDING SEASON.

While most birds are more territorial during the breeding season when they are seeking mates and defending preferred feeding or nesting sites, in the non-breeding season birds that don't migrate will often join mixed flocks of similar bird species, such as tits and nuthatches flocking together. These larger groups are better able to stay alert for hungry winter predators and use their extra pairs of eyes to seek out food sources to feed the flock. To prevent too much competition, many birds in these mixed flocks have slightly different feeding preferences – different foraging patterns in trees, for example – so that they don't compete with one another directly when food is at its scarcest.

HAVE BOLDER PERSONALITIES.

Many birds that stay in the same location year-round have stronger personalities and show more curiosity and intelligence than migratory birds. These qualities help non-migrants learn to investigate new food sources, seek out shelter, and stay alert to predators more successfully than calmer species. These birds tend to be more opportunistic, and will take advantage of new resources that other birds might overlook.

The exact species of migratory and non-migratory birds in a region depends on different factors. In general, tropical regions with milder temperatures and less disparity between seasons will have fewer migratory species. On the other hand, regions with more extreme seasons and more pronounced shifts from abundance to scarcity tend to have higher proportions of migratory species with fewer hardy species that stay in the area year-round.

There are species in nearly every scientific bird family classification that do not migrate, and every point on the planet is home to non-migratory birds – just as every point is also home to migratory birds on some stage of their annual migration cycle. Many species of chickadees, tits, woodpeckers, owls, grouse, quail, ptarmigan, pheasants, jays, magpies, doves and nuthatches are among the birds that don't typically follow long-distance migrations, delighting both birders and non-birders alike throughout the year in their home ranges.

Rock Ptarmigan
(*Lagopus muta*)

COMMON RINGED PLOVER ♂♀
(Charadrius hiaticula)

TYPE OF MIGRATION:
Seasonal, Latitudinal, Leap-frog

The common ringed plover is a familiar shorebird found during the summer along coasts, tidal flats and open tundra from Greenland to the Chukchi Peninsula in northeastern Russia, with some breeding populations as far south as the United Kingdom and northern France. While the broadly distributed northern population travels to the north African coast, the Arabian peninsula and sub-Saharan Africa, the populations in the UK, Ireland and France do not generally migrate.

This leap-frog pattern gives non-migratory birds an advantage because they do not have to travel extensively to and from breeding grounds, and can potentially have greater nesting success. Ornithologists are continually studying this disjointed migration to determine if the migratory and non-migratory bird populations should really be split into separate species. Migration, however, is only one factor in determining species status.

CAN MIGRATING BIRDS SLEEP IN FLIGHT?

Migratory flights can be exhausting, especially when birds travel hundreds or even thousands of kilometres in just a few weeks. Many birds will take advantage of stopover habitats to rest up along the way, but what about when they're migrating over broad oceans, inland seas or large lakes, and there's no place to land and give their wings a rest?

Many seabirds, such as albatrosses and petrels, as well as waterfowl like geese, ducks and swans, are able to land on the surface of the water for a break. But other birds cannot stay afloat as easily and don't have this option. Instead, birds such as thrushes, warblers, hummingbirds, sandpipers, martins and larks are able to sleep in mid-flight even as they continue their journey. What they do is enter a resting state known as unihemispheric slow-wave sleep (USWS), where just one-half of their brain is at low function while the other half remains aware and alert. This allows them to mentally rest and recharge each side of their brain at different times, while the other side continues to monitor flight conditions, adjust navigation and watch for predators or other threats. Birds may enter USWS for just a few seconds or up to several minutes at a time, taking a number of 'power naps' throughout their long flights. Several species have been studied for USWS, including the peregrine falcon (*Falco peregrinus*), Alpine swift (*Tachymarptis melba*), great frigatebird (*Fregata minor*) and Eurasian blackbird (*Turdus merula*).

When exactly birds sleep in flight is also critical, and research has shown that they are much more likely to enter USWS only while soaring on warming air currents that provide adequate lift and buoyancy in flight. This ensures that the half-sleeping bird is supported as it naps, without risk of faltering in the air and plunging into the water.

Studies have also shown that birds sleep much less than anticipated while in flight, and may have fewer than 50 minutes of USWS sleep during a 24-hour period. In contrast, the same birds may sleep for several hours after they reach land and are able to safely roost, which emphasizes the critical importance of preserving appropriate habitats at stopover sites.

MYTHS ABOUT MIGRATION

The idea that all birds migrate is one of the most enduring myths about migration. Despite the fact that we now know a great deal about bird migration, our past understanding of it has been riddled with legends, lore and fantasy. When we first became aware that birds disappeared and reappeared in a seasonal pattern, it seemed an outrageous and impossible proposal that a small bird – only a few centimetres long and weighing just a few grams – might travel hundreds or thousands of kilometres and safely return after several months. The most learned minds of different cultures and civilizations sought to explain birds' mysterious habits in different ways, with proposals, theories and declarations that can seem ludicrous today.

The Greek philosopher Aristotle, undeniably one of the greatest philosophical minds in history, proposed that birds metamorphosed into different species between seasons. His observations of moulting birds, coupled with the timing of different species' migrations, led him to declare that the common redstart (*Phoenicurus phoenicurus*) transmogrified into the European robin (*Erithacus rubecula*). The fact that the two birds were not seen at the same time and their similar sizes and colourations supported the theory. While the idea is preposterous today, it does show that bird migration has fascinated scholars for more than 2,000 years.

An even less logical but still widely accepted theory in its time was first proposed by Swedish archbishop Olaus Magnus in the 1500s. Having seen swallows congregating in marshlands and along rivers just before they disappeared for the season, Magnus believed they dived into the water to burrow into the mud beneath rivers and lakes in order to hibernate until spring. The hibernation of mammals was already well understood, and so it was a reasonable hypothesis that birds would hibernate as well. This theory also chimed with the ideas of Aristotle, who had similarly proposed that birds hibernate – although he believed they sought refuge in hollow trees or holes in the ground, rather than underwater.

PURPLE MARTIN ♂
(Progne subis)

TYPE OF MIGRATION:
Seasonal, Latitudinal

Like many swifts, swallows and martins, the purple martin was once believed to hibernate, change form, or even disappear beneath lakes and rivers after its breeding season rather than migrate long distances. While we no longer believe these impossible stories, the purple martin's long distance migration is nearly as impossible to believe. These birds travel between North America and South America as far as from Canada to Argentina, and gather in large staging flocks for days or weeks before starting on their journeys. Several thousand martins, even hundreds of thousands, may gather in the same roost before migrating, and the same roost locations will be used year after year as the birds get ready for their travels. The oldest purple martins, either male or female, begin migration earlier, with younger birds following slightly later. While these birds do gather in flocks both before migration as well as at their colonial nesting sites, they are actually independent and do not migrate strictly as a group.

♂ *Common Poorwill*
(Phalaenoptilus nuttallii)

Today, we know that most birds do not distinctively hibernate. The common poorwill (*Phalaenoptilus nuttallii*) is the only bird that hibernates, sleeping away the winter in caves and rocky crevices in its native range in northern Mexico and southwestern United States. However, many bird species do enter a short-term torpor state that's similar to hibernation. While in torpor, birds can lower their metabolism to conserve energy until conditions improve, and appear to be sleeping, but this state is only viable for a few hours and not sustainable for an entire season. Birds such as hummingbirds, swifts, frogmouths, chickadees and nighthawks will use torpor overnight or during extreme cold snaps, but will revive within a few hours to resume their normal activities.

The misconception of bird hibernation persisted for centuries, and remained a popular migration myth until the 1800s. Other theories, though, were even more outrageous, and proposed by some prominent leaders in the scientific community.

Charles Morton, an English scientist and minister in the late 1600s who would become the first vice president of Harvard College in 1697, developed the theory that birds migrated seasonally, but not to other continents. Instead, Morton believed birds migrated to the moon. At the time, the wintering ranges of the birds he studied were unknown, and Morton combined his study of bird movements with other elements of natural philosophy and the scientific method to support his theory. He believed birds were able to make such a tremendous journey because they would not be affected by gravity along the way, thus easing their flight, and allowing them to sleep en route. This hypothesis was part of the science and scientific method teachings developed by Morton and followed at both Harvard and Yale from the late 1680s to the 1720s.

Myths continue to pervade our understanding of birds' seasonal movements to this day. One of the most incredulous bits of modern bird migration folklore is that small birds hitch rides with larger birds to make their journeys. For example, it has long been believed that the tiny goldcrest (*Regulus regulus*) rode on the back of the more robust Eurasian woodcock (*Scolopax rusticola*) in order to migrate across the often treacherous North Sea between Scandinavia and the United Kingdom. Likewise, it remains an old wives' tale that the diminutive ruby-throated hummingbird (*Archilochus colubris*) hitchhikes on the backs of Canada geese (*Branta canadensis*) to make its migration across the Gulf of Mexico, a nonstop journey of 1,500 kilometres (930 miles) that seems impossible for a bird just 9 centimetres (3.5 inches) long to make without assistance.

Of course, neither of these species hitchhikes, and their assumed rides do not migrate through the same habitats, at the same times, or at the same altitudes as the proposed passengers. Yet it is testament to how extraordinary different aspects of bird migration can be that these legends still retain some elements of credibility.

However, the single most pervasive – and dangerous – myth about modern bird migration that remains widespread today is the idea that feeding migratory birds keeps them from migrating, causing them to succumb to the changing seasons. In fact the opposite is more accurate: offering healthy, nutritious foods to migrating birds can help them prepare for their journeys or refuel along their routes, and thus allows more birds to migrate successfully in each annual cycle.

THE FUTURE OF MIGRATION

Our understanding of migration has changed tremendously over the centuries, and it is sure to continue doing so. Further studies using more detailed mapping methodology, satellite tracking of tagged birds, drone-operated equipment, and techniques as yet unknown help us further unravel how, why, when and where birds make their amazing journeys. Yet even as we increase our understanding, we are also becoming aware of how migration itself is changing and evolving as birds adapt to the shifting world.

Due to the ever accelerating effects of climate change, plants and insects are now flourishing earlier in spring, but the solar and stellar clues that trigger bird migration do not keep pace with such changes, and migratory birds may be missing out on the most abundant food resources that support their migration instincts. However, some birds are already known to be migrating earlier in spring and later in autumn to compensate for these food resource shifts and climatic changes.

Over time, extreme climate change may help extend the breeding season for some bird species, allowing more broods to mature and greater population growth and breeding success. But the same change could put other birds further out of sync with essential resources, shortening their breeding season and decreasing populations. Different species will adapt to these changes differently. Birds with the longest migration journeys are perhaps most vulnerable and may have less ability to adapt over time. In contrast, those with shorter migrations might be more successful and more easily adapt to even sudden changes.

Depending on how much the climate changes and how quickly those changes occur, other shifts in bird migratory patterns could be seen, including:

- Changes in which birds claim which breeding sites, such as leks, rookeries and prime nesting locations, perhaps denying the same sites to other species.

- Shifts in which birds compete for which resources at different times in the season, and when those resources are most available.

- A shortening or lengthening of the distances migratory
  birds have to travel between suitable ranges, perhaps
  requiring more safe stopover habitats and better food
  to fuel their journeys.

As climate change continues – and it will continue, just as
ice ages, continental drift and other geological processes
naturally change the climate over different periods of time
– even birds' migration routes will change. As sea levels
rise, coastlines will shift, and birds that once migrated
directly across broad waterways may have to switch to
coastal routes in order to manage ever more incredible
migratory distances.

Birds that migrate over mountains may find that as those peaks grow – and the world's fastest growing individual mountain, Nanga Parbat in northern Pakistan's Himalayas, is growing at approximately 7 millimetres (0.27 inches) per year – they need to shift to travelling around them or through valleys instead. Similarly, birds that migrate over shrinking mountains – peaks that are growing shorter as glaciers diminish or erosion wears them away – may also switch to new routes. Changing routes means changes in migration timings, which alters the lengths of breeding seasons, affects the food sources birds can take advantage of, and requires birds to be continually adaptable to succeed in their ongoing travels.

The only certain thing we know about the future of bird migration is that it will change. Birds can and do adapt to many changes, however, and we can help them do so.

YOUR ROLE IN BIRD MIGRATION

Humans have a great impact on bird migration. Too often, though, that impact is a negative one with invasive predators, litter, pollution, urban development, poaching and other problems all threatening migrating birds. But it's easy to have a much more positive influence on bird migration by following a few simple steps that can help all birds, from common thrushes, finches and sparrows to more exotic flamingos, puffins and raptors, migrate successfully.

PROVIDE FRESH WATER

Just as migrating birds need nutritious foods to fuel their journeys, they also require clean, fresh water. This isn't just for drinking – they also need it for bathing and preening in order to keep their feathers in top condition for more aerodynamic flight. Bird baths ought to be no more than 2.5–5 centimetres (1–2 inches) deep to accommodate birds of all sizes. Broader, sturdy basins will help flocks feel more comfortable, as well as providing space for larger birds to splash about.

If space permits, even more elaborate water features will help attract more birds' attention, especially those just passing through that may not notice a smaller, simpler bird bath. Moving water, such as a fountain or a waterfall spilling into a small pond, will draw great interest with its sparkles and splashes, while a small stream is even better for giving many birds a safe, attractive watering spot.

BAR-HEADED GOOSE ♂♀
(Anser indicus)

TYPE OF MIGRATION:
Seasonal, Latitudinal

The bar-headed goose is a high-altitude champion. Whereas many birds navigate around tall mountains or funnel their migration through available passes, these geese fly straight over the Himalayas, the tallest mountain range on earth. They have even been seen flying directly over Mount Everest. The highest altitude they have been recorded at is 10,050 metres (33,000 feet), and they can complete a 1,600-kilometre (1,000-mile) migration in just one day.

The hypothesis is that these geese have adapted to their migration over eons, beginning with lower-altitude migrations before the range – which is still rising by roughly 1 centimetre (0.4 inches) per year – was quite so tall. As the mountains grew, the birds simply evolved more efficient and larger lungs, stronger muscles and more enriched blood to complete their phenomenal journey.

ADOPT BIRD-FRIENDLY LANDSCAPING

Even a single garden or yard can be a welcome oasis for migrating birds, especially in urban and suburban areas where wild habitats are continually disappearing. Bird-friendly landscaping that incorporates native plants providing familiar foods such as blooms, berries, nuts and seeds, as well as safe shelter, is essential to assist migratory birds. Pruning should be minimized, or at least delayed until after peak migration periods, to help retain a more natural environment more welcoming to birds.

Even better than landscaping a single yard is to incorporate bird-friendly practices on a larger scale in public parks and gardens, as well as in businesses, schools, churches and other sites. Many locations will welcome volunteer assistance and suggestions for maintaining landscaping, and when the work involved also helps benefit birds and other local wildlife, everyone prospers.

FEED BIRDS NUTRITIOUSLY

The better nutrition wild birds receive, the healthier they will be and the better chance they will have of completing their migrations safely. Offer the best possible foods, from sunflower seeds to suet and fruits, at feeders and feeding stations and plant natural foods for birds to comfortably forage. During peak migration periods, putting out foods with higher fat and calories, such as suet or nuts, will help birds refuel more quickly and give them more energy for their extended travels.

As much as possible, avoid less nutritious foods such as breads, cakes, cookies, crisps and other products high in empty carbohydrates. While these can fill birds' bellies, they do not provide adequate nutrition to maintain the strong muscles, vibrant nerves and swift reflexes that help birds migrate successfully.

CLEAN FEEDERS AND BATHS

Offering feeders full of nutritious seeds and baths brimming with water undoubtedly helps migrating birds, but these resources can be damaging, or even deadly, if not properly maintained. Unless they're regularly cleaned, feeders and baths can quickly accumulate layers of faeces, rotting hulls and mouldy food, as well as algae growth and insect infestations. These can spread diseases to birds that visit, which in turn may be carried along the migration route to infect the rest of a flock or delicate nesting area.

Regular cleaning and sterilizing with a weak bleach solution can easily prevent such contamination. Feeders should be wiped out every time they're refilled, with more thorough cleanings every one to two weeks or whenever dirt has accumulated. Bird baths should be thoroughly cleaned each week, or more often in hot weather when bacteria and algae grow more quickly in the warm, standing water.

125

TURN LIGHTS OFF

Excess lighting is a well-known threat to migrating birds and can easily lead to disorientation, exhaustion or starvation as birds struggle to find their way. Turning off landscape lighting, porch lights, patio lights and lights in pools and fountains will help birds navigate more easily. If it's not possible to completely extinguish lights for safety or security reasons, switch to lower wattage bulbs or install motion-activated lights to minimize the distraction to migrating birds.

As well as turning off lights at home, encourage local businesses to get involved with lights-out programmes, particularly during peak spring and autumn migration seasons. Office buildings and parking lots often use excessive nighttime illumination, and even reducing it by a fraction can significantly help migrating birds. Not only will this help birds find their way, but it can also help businesses realize hefty energy cost savings.

MINIMIZE OR ELIMINATE PESTICIDES

Too often we rely on chemicals to rid our homes, yards and gardens of undesirable pests, including rodents and insects. But these same undesirables are prime foods for many birds, including flycatchers, warblers, hummingbirds, thrushes and raptors. As birds are migrating, they need these food sources to refuel, and if we avoid rodenticides, insecticides and traps, birds will happily serve as natural pest controllers.

If such chemicals absolutely must be used, they should always be applied properly and responsibly. Avoid overuse or misuse that could not only destroy food sources, but also generate toxicity levels that will harm birds, contaminate waterways and cause additional environmental problems. The same precautions should be followed for all outdoor chemicals, including herbicides and fertilizers – less is better and none is best, allowing a natural balance to develop for every yard and garden.

KEEP CATS INDOORS

Free-roaming cats, whether they are outdoor pets, strays, abandoned pets or feral cats, are one of the most damaging and destructive invasive predators worldwide, responsible for billions of bird deaths each year. Hunting cats can be especially dangerous to migratory birds because they are not expected, native predators and weary, hungry birds may be less conscientious about looking out for such threats. A cat's natural instinct is to stalk and pounce, so owners should take steps to keep birds and other wildlife away from their pet's claws and fangs. Cats should be kept strictly indoors, or if outdoor breaks are necessary, they should be closely supervised or offered a cat patio – a 'catio' – as a safe, comfortable alternative.

In areas that seem overrun with free-roaming cats, stronger measures may be necessary to protect birds. Providing secure shelter for birds to retreat from hunting cats is critical, and baffles should be used to keep cats from reaching feeding stations or nest boxes where migrating birds may take refuge. Supporting local cat shelters, as well as responsible pet ownership, can also help reduce free-roaming cats and protect birds.

CLEAN UP LOCAL HABITATS

Small yards, private gardens and groomed landscapes are only a fraction of the habitats that birds, particularly migrants, rely on for survival. As well as keeping personal property bird-friendly, it's critical to clean up more diverse local habitats such as parks, nature reserves, wetlands, sports fields, beaches, greenways and even roadsides in open countryside or woodland. Organize or join a clean-up event, participate in efforts to remove invasive plants or predators, or simply pick up litter whenever you are visiting a bird habitat that might need a little help.

Even better are preemptive efforts to avoid habitat damage in the first place. Be sure to properly secure and dispose of your own trash, recycle whenever possible, discard broken fishing line safely, maintain your vehicle to prevent toxic fluid leaks, and teach others to similarly respect habitats that provide crucial stopover sites for migratory birds.

MAKE WINDOWS VISIBLE

Billions of birds die from window collisions worldwide each year, and peak migration periods are the most dangerous time for birds interacting with these deadly obstacles. Birds cannot see glass clearly and often mistake reflections of the sky or nearby plants on hard, unforgiving panes for a safe flying route or welcoming perch. Even if a collision is not immediately fatal, a stunned bird is more vulnerable to nearby predators or may succumb to internal injuries, thirst or starvation before it can sufficiently recover.

To help birds see windows, install simple cling decals, frosted tape strips or cutout shapes on the glass (outside is best, but inside is still helpful), positioning them just 5–7.5 centimetres (2–3 inches) apart so birds don't try to fly through the perceived gaps. Closing shutters, reducing interior lights, installing exterior screens, or even leaving glass a bit dirtier can all help minimize glare and help birds see the glass as the obstacle it is. These steps should not just be taken on homes, but on any building with broad windows or glassy surfaces, including schools, offices, hospitals, libraries and other public sites.

INTRODUCE OTHERS TO BIRDS

One of the simplest, most effective ways you can help bird migration is to share your interest with others. Introducing friends and family to birds and spreading enthusiasm about migration will encourage even more people to take a positive role. While one individual may be able to take five good steps to support migration, if they can also get five friends, family members, neighbours or coworkers to notice and appreciate migrating birds, that could add up to 25 more steps being taken. And if each of those people then introduces five of their acquaintances to birds, that could amount to more than 150 steps in support of migration, with no end in sight. There's no upper limit to the help that can be offered if more and more people get involved in simple ways.

To spread the word about birds and migration even more, consider offering a migration-themed lecture at a local library, talking to a school class about how to help birds, or posting informational signs in your office or workplace to get more people positively involved.

FIELDFARE ♂♀

(Turdus pilaris)

TYPE OF MIGRATION:
Seasonal, Latitudinal, Longitudinal, Leap-frog, Nomadic

The attractive fieldfare is an easily recognized thrush, with birders and non-birders alike noting its movements as it migrates in spring and autumn, its arrival or departure often coinciding with the change of seasons. Not all fieldfares migrate, however, and a central core of their range is occupied year-round. When the birds do undertake their annual journeys, they do so en masse, often moving in tremendous flocks that

can number 1,000 birds or more. Younger birds that migrate typically travel shorter distances, gradually lengthening their migrations with age and experience. Even outside of migration periods, fieldfares can be slightly nomadic, wandering in search of abundant foods, especially berries and fruits in winter after insect populations have dwindled.

GREATER FLAMINGO ♂♀
(Phoenicopterus roseus)

TYPE OF MIGRATION:
*Seasonal, Longitudinal,
Nomadic, Dispersal*

The greater flamingo is great indeed in its migration. Not only does it have the widest distribution of all the world's flamingo species, but it also occupies the most diverse range of habitats. Its migration is similarly diverse, and while not all greater flamingos migrate, those that do have a variety of migration adaptations. Northern and western populations migrate seasonally, while populations in temperate, year-round regions are more nomadic and will migrate when water levels aren't

suitable for feeding or breeding; when there's too much competition for nesting space within a large colony; or when food levels can't support so many birds. This can make the greater flamingo's migration more erratic, but when they soar in large, dramatic flocks, it's a sight well worth seeing – if you can, that is, as greater flamingos typically migrate at night. After they mature, juvenile flamingos also undertake modest dispersal migrations to find their own mates and ranges.

ENJOYING MIGRATION

One of the very best ways to get involved in bird migration and help all birds making their tremendous journeys is simply to enjoy migration yourself. As you discover more passing migrants, you will naturally take more steps to encourage and protect them, as well as to share that excitement with others and hopefully spark their own migration enthusiasm. But enjoying migration is so much more.

Visit a nature centre, wildlife reserve or wild-bird refuge. Not only will you see migratory birds that might not visit your garden or home habitats, but your name and address on the sign-in sheet or visitor log will show the popularity of the facility and help support funding efforts for further habitat preservation. Any entrance fees, parking tolls or similar charges will likewise help support the facility or network of facilities, as will any money you spend on purchasing souvenirs, visiting a refreshment stand, or joining a local reserve's membership rolls.

Many local bird and wildlife festivals are timed to take advantage of peak migration periods, or local nature guides and conservationists may offer guided walks or tours during these times to see what birds are passing by at different moments. Join these walks or participate in festivals to learn more about local migratory species, or use events further afield as an opportunity to travel and take in more migratory wonders.

At the same time, don't miss the migration going on right in your own backyard or garden. Take time each day to peer into the shrubbery, study the treetops, or simply watch a feeding station and see what birds are visiting. As the seasons change, so will the visitors, with some guests continuing their migration routes and others settling in for a seasonal residency. It can be very revealing and rewarding to keep a personal calendar, journal, notebook or checklist of bird visits and movements, and reviewing those notes in later years can help you make startling revelations about just how punctual and predictable migrants can be, or how their travel patterns change over time.

The more we enjoy and explore migration, the more we will learn about it and understand not only how birds accomplish this amazing feat, but also how we can help them along on their remarkable journeys.

Together, let's fly.

FURTHER READING

Every time a bird spreads its wings, there is more we can learn about migration. These fine resources will help you along the way:

The Migration of Birds: Seasons on the Wing (Janice M. Hughes; Firefly Books, 2009)

Flight Lines: Tracking the Wonders of Bird Migration (Mike Toms; British Trust for Ornithology, 2017)

Long Hops: Making Sense of Bird Migration (Mark Denny; Latitude 20, 2016)

Atlas of Bird Migration: Tracing the Great Journeys of the World's Birds (Jonathan Elphick; Firefly Books, 2011)

Many journals and magazines devoted to birds also regularly feature migration articles and insights:

- *Birds & Blooms* (birdsandblooms.com)
- *Birds & Blooms* EXTRA! (birdsandblooms.com)
- *BirdWatching* (US) (birdwatchingdaily.com)
- *Bird Watching* (UK) (birdwatching.co.uk)
- *Birdwatch* (birdguides.com)

Your favourite local, national and international conservation organizations, including the Royal Society for the Protection of Birds, the National Audubon Society and BirdLife International also publish materials related to bird migration, including ongoing research and new studies. Memberships for these and other organizations often include subscriptions to their newsletters or magazines and access to their research on all types of bird topics.

FURTHER READING

BE A CHAMPION FOR MIGRATORY BIRDS

The more we learn about bird migration, the more we are inspired to help birds safely complete their epic journeys. There is no more helpful and inspirational way to do so than to support Champions of the Flyway.

Founded in 2014, this annual event has raised more than £320,000 ($420,000) to support various bird conservation projects throughout Europe, Africa and the Middle East, all connected via the Mediterranean flyway through Israel. Various teams raise funds and race through a big day event to see as many bird species in southern Israel as possible, raising awareness of conservation efforts every step of the way. Awards are given to teams that not only see the greatest number of species and raise the most money for each year's conservation action project, but also for the team that best promotes the cause before, during and after the event. Teams are encouraged to share sightings and tips during race day, fostering cooperation typically unheard of in competitive events. Furthermore, race organizers ensure that birds' safety is of the greatest importance throughout the day's challenge, and teams are prohibited from disturbing the region's most sensitive and vulnerable species.

While Champions of the Flyway is focused on protecting migratory birds in the Mediterranean region, its organizers also work with other bodies to inspire and design similar events elsewhere in the world. This spreads the message of conservation and cooperation far beyond the borders of any one country or continent, and helps protect all migratory birds no matter their ranges or travelling routes.

To help support Champions of the Flyway, a portion of the sales from *Migration: Exploring the Remarkable Journeys of Birds* will be donated to the event each year, and each copy purchased will help support those donations and keep migratory birds in flight. For more information about Champions of the Flyway, visit champions-of-the-flyway.com, and for details about *Migration*'s donations, visit BeYourOwnBirder.com.

INDEX

ABOUT THE AUTHOR

As a birder, Melissa Mayntz has seen hundreds of species, witnessed astonishing seasonal migrations, and attracted dozens of bird species to her yard. Her work has previously appeared in *National Wildlife* magazine, Bird Watcher's Digest Online, Watching Backyard Birds, TheSpruce.com, and *WildBird*, among other publications. Find her online at MelissaMayntz.com and BeYourOwnBirder.com.

ACKNOWLEDGEMENTS

This book has not been a solo migration by any means. Great thanks and awe are due to Harriet Butt, my ever patient, enthusiastic and encouraging editor at Quadrille Publishing, for not only seeing the potential for this work, but for helping ease it along at every step, no matter how I may have faltered on those steps along the way. Katy Christianson also deserves props and kudos for bringing black-and-white words to colourful illustrated life and stunning perspective on every page, helping the birds fly throughout this book.

The entire Quadrille team – Nicola, Nick, Katie, Maeve and countless others who've been involved in pitch meetings, layout, design, editing, fact-checking, indexing, scheduling, and more – must be thanked profusely. Without the entire flock, this book would never have gotten off the ground.

To every bird I've seen, every bird I've enjoyed, and every bird I still seek out on all my own journeys, I also owe my gratitude. Without them I'd never have been inspired to write about birds at all. I promise to refill the feeders more often.

To all my birdy clients and all the work they've collected over the years, and to my birdy friends and readers whom I've met on all types of migrations – thank you for your belief in the words I share and the skill I am never able to see, and for helping to spread my writing to others. Your flock is far too large, diverse and widespread to be named in these few sentences, and even pages and pages of thanks wouldn't be enough to express my profound appreciation.

For Trevor, just because.

And to my husband, Marc, whose support, love and partnership has always been phenomenal and unwavering. Without you none of this would be. My thanks, my love and my heart is always yours.